# YOU TOO CAN BE CHACHA CHAUDHARY

Dr. Vinod Sharma



DIAMOND BOOKS
www.diamondbooks.in

**Publisher** : **Diamond Pocket Books (P) Ltd.**
X-30, Okhla Industrial Area,
Phase-II, New Delhi-110020
Phone : 011-40712200
E-mail : wecare@diamondbooks.in
Website : www.diamondbooks.in
Edition : 2025

---

**YOU TOO CAN BE CHACHA CHAUDHARY**
Author - *Dr. Vinod Sharma*

*With blessings of MAA SARASWATI,*
*I dedicate this book to my parents, my wife*
*Megha and my son Ayaan.*

*Tribute with respect and special thanks*
*to the key inspiration of this book*
*-Shri Pran Kumar Sharma*

*Many thanks and regards to our ideal, Chairman of Diamond Books- Shri Narender Kumar Verma Sir for his valuable guidance and motivation in writing of this book.*

*Many thanks to Mrs Alka Dhal and Dr Nalini Anand for their great support in translation and editing of this book.*

*Special thanks to Mr Dhruv Suwalka, Mr Rajnish Suwalka and whole Brainywood family for their constant motivation, support and blessings.*

# Preface

As kids, we would rush to the shop at the back street, every day when Dad used to give us some money, and we used to buy *Chacha Chaudhary* comics. Without reading them, our days were incomplete. Chacha Chaudhary had become an integral part of our daily routine, almost like a respected elder in the family, always present in our imaginations. Those were the days—running away from studies, eagerly waiting to dive into the world of comics.

We kids would read one line repeatedly, shouting together: *"Chacha Chaudhary's brain works faster than a computer!"* Reading those comics made us feel as if our brains had also become like his—sharp and extraordinary. For a little while, we would bask in the feeling of being just like Chacha Chaudhary, proudly imagining ourselves as quick-witted as him. Then, we'd save up whatever money we could and eagerly wait for the next comic in the series.

Sooner or later, Mom's voice would ring out, asking us to sit down and study. And as we opened our textbooks, the stark difference between Chacha Chaudhary's brain and ours would become painfully clear. His brain might work faster than a computer, but ours? It seemed more like a cheap tape recorder that couldn't even retain what our teacher said in class. Alongside Chacha Chaudhary, our thoughts would wander to Grandma too, as studying felt dull, and focus seemed impossible.

Yet, after hours of exhausting studying, picking up *Chacha Chaudhary* comics again felt like a reward. That line—*"Chacha*

*Chaudhary's brain works faster than a computer!"*—would once again make us proud of ourselves, if only for a fleeting moment.

A question often came to mind: *Why does Chacha Chaudhary's brain work faster than a computer? How does it work like that? Could our brain ever be like his?* Reading Chacha Ji's comics was so much fun, but why did our own studies feel so dull and boring?

As we grew older, comics slowly faded into the background, and life moved forward. Yet, whenever life presented a challenge, the thought always crossed my mind: *If only my brain worked like Chacha Chaudhary's—sharp and fast like a computer—I could solve any problem instantly.*

I often wondered how Chacha Chaudhary's brain worked so quickly. What was the secret formula that made it possible? Could I discover that secret someday? If I could unlock that mystery, maybe my brain could also function like his—capable of tackling every problem with ease and solving every challenge effortlessly.

A physically frail and lean elder like Chacha Ji can easily conquer towering, massive challenges because of his extraordinary mind. Imagine if we had such a brain; life would be so much more enjoyable.

Now, after so many years, it feels like I've come across several ideas and methods that, if applied, could help anyone—every child, every person—train their mind to work just as efficiently as Chacha Chaudhary's. Perhaps, with the right approach, everyone could develop a brain as sharp as his.

The most important thing is that the mind is the key to success in this world. It is the greatest tool given to us by God. Just as working out and exercising can make the body strong and powerful, the same applies to the mind. If we work on our mind, engage in mental exercises, challenge it regularly, and uncover the secrets to sharpening it—learning, understanding, and internalizing those techniques—the mind, too, can become powerful and extraordinary.

In life, who finds the solution to every problem? The mind. Life essentially presents us with two things: problems and solutions. A problem is a situation, while a solution is our response to it.

When we face a situation, we must respond to it, and this response depends on the capacity of our mind. Our behaviour, what we have learned, our IQ level, and our understanding determine the nature of our response.

Broadly, there are two types of responses: **instinctive** and **controlled.** Instinctive responses are similar in all living beings. Animals, for instance, give instinctive reactions. However, humans have the unique ability to train their minds to manage and control their responses, giving **controlled reactions.**

Controlled responses are the key to success and happiness. They are the foundation, the secret, and the guiding principle of achieving great outcomes in life.

While situations are often beyond our control, our responses to them are entirely within our control. And therein lies the power of the mind—to shape our lives, our success, and our satisfaction. We may not have control over a situation, but how we behave or react to that situation is entirely within our control.

Birds, animals, and other creatures respond instinctively. However, humans, through education, learning, behaviour, and life experiences, can shape their minds to provide controlled responses based on what they have learned and understood.

This ability to give controlled reactions was the unique quality of Chacha Chaudhary's mind. He would analyse, evaluate, and understand a situation instantly, responding with the most ideal, appropriate, and effective solution.

If everyone could adopt this trait or learn this skill, life would become truly delightful. It would simplify life, align it to our preferences, and bring success and happiness firmly under our control.

Let's understand instinctive and controlled responses with an example. Imagine you have an important task to complete, and you need to step out of the house, but it's raining heavily outside. One possible reaction could be to cancel your plan, thinking, "It's raining, I'll get wet," and decide to postpone the important work. Another reaction could be to step out without any preparation, get completely drenched, feel uncomfortable, and possibly even fall sick. Being wet and distracted might also cause you to handle the task inefficiently.

The third and most thoughtful reaction would be to prepare for the rain by taking an umbrella or wearing a raincoat before stepping out. This way, you can complete your work without getting wet or uncomfortable, and there's no need to delay your task.

This example shows how a **controlled response** helps us handle a situation efficiently. By analysing the situation, finding a practical solution, and acting thoughtfully, we can respond in the best possible way. In this case, the umbrella or raincoat becomes the symbol of preparation and a logical approach to overcoming the challenge of the rain. When it starts raining, animals and birds instinctively leave everything behind and run for cover to protect themselves. On the other hand, humans can continue working because of their ability to prepare and adapt. But who created the umbrella or invented the raincoat that enables us to deal with such situations? It was the human mind that analysed the problem, found a solution, and came up with these inventions.

In fact, every invention in the world is essentially a solution to a problem—a result of a **controlled response** to challenges. A scientific mindset focuses on solutions rather than dwelling on problems. Scientists enjoy tackling challenges, finding opportunities within difficulties, and creating solutions that make life easier.

Chacha Chaudhary used to approach even the toughest problems with a sense of joy. In difficult situations, he would make the best use of his mind to find solutions, always treating them as opportunities. Every time, he learned something new and kept moving forward. This mental response became a major characteristic of his sharp intellect, and we would often hear that Chacha Chaudhary's mind works faster than a computer. What does a computer do? It collects information, processes it, and then turns it into a function. First, it receives the information, and then, using different software, it converts it into reactions and actions. The human mind works in a similar way. It gathers information through our senses—touch, smell, hearing, sight, and taste. After that, based on our behaviour, past learning, IQ level, and how we think and understand, the brain processes this information. It reacts, stores it, and gives instructions to use the information when needed. However, the level of your mind affects your functions and reactions significantly. To make the mind powerful and sharp, we can learn many things from Chacha Chaudhary.

In this book, we have tried to include lessons from his life that can benefit a small child, a student, family members, parents, and an ordinary person. The goal is for future generations, especially children, to develop a mind like Chacha Chaudhary's. If they can find solutions to the problems they face in their studies through their own minds, and receive strong motivation and solutions for every challenge they encounter in life, then every child and every person can develop a mindset, perspective, and behaviour like Chacha Chaudhary's. With the right attitude and controlled responses, many problems can be solved, leading to the creation of a progressive, ideal society and nation.

This book, inspired by the ideal life of Chacha Chaudhary and the many lessons we can learn from him, is dedicated to the creator of Chacha Chaudhary, Cartoonist Pran Kumar Sharma (1938-2014) aka 'Pran'. We salute all the readers who have enjoyed Chacha Chaudhary's comics till now. It is also dedicated to our esteemed Chairman of Diamond Books, Shri Narender Kumar Verma, and the entire Diamond Books team.

This book aims to convey the inspiration and lessons from Chacha Chaudhary's life, especially for students, children, and family members. Let us enjoy, understand, and strive to bring the qualities of Chacha Ji's character and personality into our own lives. We should also make an effort to see if we too can have a mind like Chacha Chaudhary's.

# Contents

LET'S SEE WHAT'S INSIDE!!

CHACHA
CHAUDHARY
KA DIMAAG
COMPUTER
SE BHI TEZ
CHALTA HAI

*Chapter 1*

# Why Does Chacha Chaudhary's Mind Work Faster Than a computer?

To understand this, we need to explore three aspects: Chacha Chaudhary himself—his personality and life values, his exceptional mind, and the unique qualities that make it faster than a computer.

The title asks: Why Does Chacha Chaudhary's Mind Work Faster Than a computer?

As we have previously understood, life revolves around two main aspects: situations and responses. The way we respond depends on what we have learned and understood in our lives—through our behaviour, family, education, and the systems we have been part of so far.

Our ability to train and elevate our mind determines the quality of our response. A controlled response is an ideal response because it is solution-focused and leads to positive outcomes.

If we align our efforts with this goal, study with focus, and train our mind in various ways, we can achieve ideal results in life. A disciplined and well-trained mind enables us to face challenges effectively and make meaningful progress.

The mind functions like a computer with two primary tasks: gathering information and then processing it based on learning.

This processed information is converted into functions, actions, or reactions as needed.

When required, the mind effectively utilizes all memories or stored data, ensuring the right response at the right time. If your computer has a powerful processor, a high-quality motherboard, efficient software, and a large-capacity hard disk, it will naturally perform well.

Additionally, the user operating the computer must also have good knowledge of how to use it effectively to maximize its potential.

So, what does a computer do? It receives a large amount of information, stores it, evaluates and processes it instantly, and then provides the results.

The brain works in a similar way. It gathers information, analyses it, and responds to situations. A situation is like a command that demands a response from us. In this analogy, we are the users of our brain, responsible for how it processes and reacts. The level of the brain's processor, its capacity, the quality of thinking and understanding, its behaviour, what it has learned, its intelligence quotient, and whether the memories stored within it are permanent or not—all these factors determine the nature of its response.

If the brain is sharp and efficient, its responses will be quick, calculations will be swift and accurate, and the reactions will be correct and ideal as well. This means that it is essential to train our reactions and refine our responses. In the same way, it is crucial to train our brain.

Whenever the human brain responds to a situation, it does so as a function of recollection or memory. In other words, it processes some data or information and transforms it into a reaction.

The brain's processes and responses are influenced by these six characteristics:

i. Interest,

ii. Emotion,

iii. Visualization,

iv. Association,

v. Creativity, and

vi. Logic.

Interest means the things we are curious about or enjoy. When we have an interest in something, our brain functions better, our memory works efficiently, and we dedicate time to it. This also enhances our understanding. Some people are interested in politics, others in music, some in mathematics, and some in sports. Based on our interests, we allocate our time accordingly. The memories formed in our brain related to these interests tend to be more permanent. The brain works more efficiently when we are interested in something. However, the problem arises when we lack interest in certain areas. For example, children often don't enjoy studying, but they are highly interested in video games, sports, music, or movies. As a result, their memory works better and their brain performs faster in these areas. They easily complete multiple levels in video games one after another, yet passing a single exam level requires months of effort and leaves them stressed repeatedly.

The biggest cause of stress is engaging in tasks we have no interest in. If we learn to develop interest in those tasks, stress can be significantly reduced.

**Emotion** refers to our feelings and sensitivities. Situations and information that directly impact our emotions create long-lasting memories. These memories become deeply ingrained in our minds and are retained as sharp recollections, influencing both our brain and life significantly. Emotions can be either **negative** or **positive**.

When emotions are negatively affected by adverse situations, the brain produces negative reactions. Conversely, when the impact is positive, the brain generates positive responses. Jumping off a mountain (committing suicide) is a **negative emotion**, but climbing a mountain, such as conquering Mount Everest, is a **positive emotion**. Engaging in tasks with **passion** is always linked to positive emotions. In life, **willpower** holds greater importance than skill. When we are determined to accomplish something, it reflects our emotions and our willpower.

Strong emotions enhance willpower. For instance, **Chacha Chaudhary's willpower** was very strong because he had excellent control over his emotions. In essence, learning to regulate our emotions is a key step toward mastering control over our mind.

Now comes **visualization**, which means receiving information in a visual form. The mind places great importance on visuals, and the most significant and lasting memories are those that are stored as images. We rarely forget things we have seen.

You might have experienced this yourself: sometimes when you meet someone, you feel like saying, *"I've seen you somewhere before, but I can't recall your name."* This is a common occurrence for many of us.

Our eyes have a greater capacity to store and recall visuals compared to the memory created through hearing. Memories formed through sight are far more permanent and powerful than those formed through hearing. This is why visuals stay with us—old memories from life remain intact, yet we often forget what we read in the newspaper just two days ago.

We remember a face because we saw it, but we forget the name because we only heard it. Therefore, whenever we do something in life, it's important to observe it with our eyes. For things we cannot see with our eyes, nature has given us the power of visualization, imagination, and creativity. Through these powers, we can "see" things in our mind's eye. Using imagination to visualize is a method of visualization itself. Chacha Chaudhary's sharp mind, permanent memory, and quick response to situations are greatly influenced by his incredible imagination.

Reading something 50 times, writing it 30 times, listening to it 20 times, and observing it just once can create the same level of memory.

Observation enhances curiosity and interest.

For instance, whenever we visit a place and observe things with our eyes, they tend to stay in our memory.

So, if we practice converting every thought in our mind into a visual form, it will not only help in creating permanent memories but also in generating a strong response. Instead of merely reading, memorizing, or repeating things over and over, if we learn to visualize them, it will have a much greater impact on our life and studies.

You must have heard or read about the book *"The Secret,"* which explains the Law of Attraction. It emphasizes that to achieve anything, you need to imagine and visualize it repeatedly in a positive manner. This visualization is a powerful tool to attract success and achieve your goals.

Whenever we are afraid, most of the fear is not in the situation itself but in our imagination. We start fearing the outcome, and we visualize what could go wrong. This increases our fear, and the possibility of stress or pressure also rises. This is usually a result of negative visualization.

But this can also be turned into a positive. We often don't intentionally try to remember things, but they still stay in our memory. However, when we try to memorize something for studying, it doesn't always stay. This shows that what we see stays in our memory more effectively and helps in our reactions.

We remember childhood events or old memories better because they were experienced through our eyes and became a part of our visual memory. On the other hand, we may forget what we read in the newspaper or the book two days ago. This shows that your memory, your brain processes, and your reactions depend on your ability to see and visualize.

The amazing thing is that nature has given us two types of vision: one is physical, like seeing with our eyes, and the other is mental, which is seeing through imagination, visualization, and creative thinking.

One thing we mentioned is that "Seeing is Believing," meaning we believe only when we see. This is a common thought and a general idea. However, exceptional individuals, like scientists or Chacha Chaudhary, who have brought about change in their lives and in society, operate differently. Their visualization is so strong that for them, the saying "Seeing is Believing" turns into "Believing is Seeing." They see what others cannot see because they believe in it first. Just like how scientists made inventions, those inventions were already in their minds, things that no one else had seen before, but they were visible to them. For example, Edison could see a glowing bulb, Einstein saw the theory of relativity, Dalton visualized the atom, the Wright brothers envisioned an airplane in their imagination, and Newton saw gravity at work. Similarly, Chacha Chaudhary could foresee solutions to every problem and the upcoming changes in life through his imagination.

In other words, if we practice visualization with positive thinking in our imagination, we can see what could be important in the future, what might bring favourable outcomes, and what we can control. This is a scientific approach. Visualization is a very important and powerful practice.

By practicing learning methods like visualization or mnemonics, even the most difficult concepts become easier to understand, and they start getting remembered. The problem of forgetting also starts improving. So, whenever you are doing any task in life, if you use visualization—whether by transforming it into an imagined visual, using real-life visuals, or any method where it exists in your mind as a visual—it becomes a strong memory, a good learning method, and is helpful in generating responses.

Now, it's time to talk about association. From the discussion on visualization, we understood that the brain works much better when we create visuals. However, there's one more thing Dr. Thorndike mentioned: having an image, being able to see something, or showing it doesn't necessarily mean we can remember it forever or use it in reactions. It becomes possible only when we associate or link them together. In other words, recalling something or using it in reactions is possible when we connect the visuals with something else.

For example, in a house, even though we see something with our own eyes, it is often difficult to find it when we need it. Sometimes, a pen is lost, keys can't be found, sketch pens disappear, or one important document is found but another is missing. When there's a problem of not finding something at the right time, it means that our thought process or memory has not been properly recollected. This indicates a problem in recalling the information effectively.

In a house, a person may be sure that an item is there because they've seen it or brought it in themselves. However, at times, even when it's within the house, it is difficult to find. Similarly, our memories or thoughts are also in our mind, and once they are there, they stay in the mind. But sometimes, they are not easily found when needed. This happens because of improper retention. And the reason for poor retention is not associating the information correctly. Good memory and proper responses will only occur when we correctly associate and link our thoughts. This is known as the Law of Association.

For example, at home, we often hear things like "the pen is lost," "the keys are missing," "the handkerchief is nowhere to be found," or "where's the TV remote?" or "the sketch pens are gone," or even "important papers are missing." But have you ever heard someone say, "The tomatoes are lost" or "The lemons are missing"? You might find this funny, because tomatoes and lemons, like any other household item, don't typically get lost. This is because they have a designated place, a logical association, which we've trained ourselves to remember, both at home and in our minds. For instance, food items go in the fridge, clothes in the wardrobe, and utensils in the kitchen. However, we tend to leave things like keys or pens lying around anywhere. Though they are still in the house, they are not found when needed. The reaction doesn't work properly, and this happens because without proper association, recall doesn't happen efficiently.

We can associate things within our visualization itself. For example, when you connect your goal with emotions and the outcome of achieving that goal, and then visualize it, your energy increases. You feel enthusiastic, the fatigue of working on that task disappears, and stress is reduced. This process of positive visualization, combined with an organized method to remember these things, can be highly effective in sharpening your mind. This is one of the unique abilities of a brain like Chacha Chaudhary's.

Now comes an important topic: **Creativity**, or innovative thinking.

Let's first understand the difference between logic and creativity. Logic is a repeatable function— a basic principle that, once learned, can be applied by anyone to replicate a process. On the other hand, **creativity** is about creating something new, something personal and unique.

Every individual has the ability to create something new; this remarkable gift has been given to us by nature. All the inventions we have seen so far are results of creativity—innovative and original thinking. Creating something that didn't exist before is the essence of creativity.

Finding solutions within problems is **creativity**.

A small child draws pictures on paper, weaves their own stories, and creates various levels in video games using their imagination and creativity, clearing them one by one. In different kinds of games, they come up with new ideas and innovations. They may unscrew old clocks or fix toys using their curious and resourceful mind. All of these are the results of their creativity.

Chacha Chaudhary's mind was highly creative. He always found unique opportunities within problems and solved them with his creativity.

About 500,000 years ago, humans and animals lived in very similar ways. Animals would leave their shelters to search for food, eat, and return to their place. Our routine was no different—we, too, left our caves in search of food, and after finding it, returned to our shelter in the evening. In essence, both humans and animals followed almost identical daily patterns.

Today, after so many years, both animals and humans have changed, but in different ways. Animals still follow the same routine—they leave their shelters in the morning, search for food, eat, and return to their place to rest.

However, humans now engage in a variety of activities. We no longer step out just to search for food. Today, we enjoy the cool breeze of air conditioning, travel in airplanes, talk on mobile phones, and make video calls with people thousands of kilometres away.

We use computers, stay online, and are surrounded by countless inventions and conveniences. All these innovations, which have made us modern, are the result of creativity.

Animals are not creative, which is why they do not create anything new—they only use what nature has provided them. However, humans are creative, and that is why, in every era, they invent something new and keep changing the world.

From the smallest problems to the biggest challenges, everything can be effectively controlled and transformed through creativity. It all depends on how creative you are and whether you have trained yourself to enhance your creativity.

Finally, we come to logic. Chacha Chaudhary had sharp logic and incredible reasoning abilities. Logic allows us to create principles for performing tasks repeatedly. It helps us simplify tasks, like mathematics, grammar, and science. These fields rely on logic, which is why they can be taught and applied repeatedly.

The key strength of logic is its reliability. People trust logic because it is based on reasoning. That's why we have faith in science, scientific facts, mathematics, and logical reasoning.

Logic means a response that makes sense to our mind or answers a question arising in our brain.

We can develop our logical thinking through various means—school education, learning from elders, observing our surroundings, reading books, studying, or staying in the company of intelligent people.

IQ (Intelligence Quotient) essentially reflects the level of your logical ability.

Chacha Chaudhary possessed an exceptionally sharp and logical mind. From him, we learn the importance of nurturing our logical abilities from a young age.

We should focus on improving our reasoning skills, engaging in thorough study, and cultivating a mindset that seeks logical solutions to every problem and situation.

With logic, reasoning, and the intelligence of the mind, even the most complex problems can be solved instantly.

Let's continue reading, where we will hear various conversations from characters like Sabu, Raka, and others from Chacha Chaudhary's comics. As a student, an individual, and a curious learner, we will explore what we can learn from Chacha Chaudhary's mind and life. From the treasure of his mind, we can gather many pearls that will help embellish our own minds.

## Functions of Brain

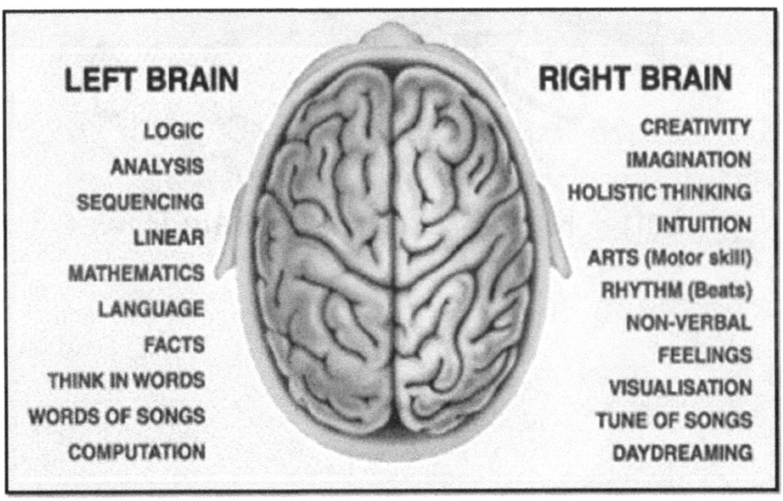

# Brain Dynamics

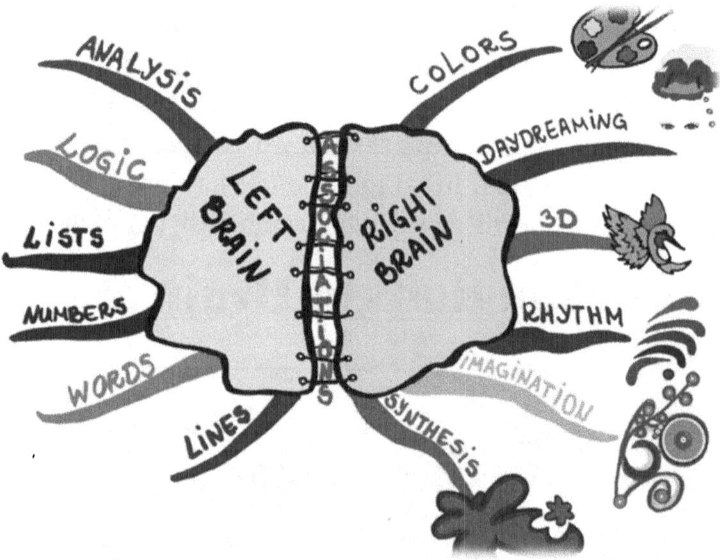


Left + Right = Expanded Brain Power

## Topic 1.1 - Power of Thinking: The Science of the Left Brain and the Magic of the Right Brain

One day, Chacha Chaudhary was reading the newspaper at home when Pinki and Raka rushed to him. They looked confused, and Pinki said, "Chacha ji, we don't understand why we can't focus properly on our studies. Sometimes we remember things, and sometimes we forget everything! And when we forget, we get scared of studying, it feels like a phobia. The fear of getting scolded adds to it. Sometimes, I wonder, who even made studying so difficult? Why do we have to study? Moreover, today we were taught that our brain has two parts. I was thinking, if our brain has two parts, then why do we still have trouble remembering our studies? But now, let's understand these two parts of the brain and study."

Chacha Chaudhary smiled, set the newspaper aside, and said, "The solution to your problem lies within our brain. Did you know that our brain is divided into two parts – the right brain and the left brain? By balancing both, we can overcome stress and fear, easily remember our studies, and even make studying more enjoyable."

Chhotu, surprised, asked, "How is that possible, Chacha ji? What is this right and left brain? And how can we make our studies easier with it?"

Chacha Chaudhary explained, "Our brain has two parts. The left brain is associated with logic, calculations, and analysis. This part helps us think logically and solve problems. On the other hand, the right brain is connected with imagination, creativity, and emotions. When we use both parts of our brain properly, stress and fear naturally disappear."

Sabu, amazed, said, "Wow, Chacha ji! So, is this all a game of the brain? Please tell me how we can use this to our advantage."

## Chacha Chaudhary's Brain Balancing Technique

Chacha Chaudhary taught the children, villagers, and everyone a unique way to balance the right and left parts of the brain. He said, "Let me teach you a brain-balancing technique. It will keep your mind calm, and you won't feel scared anymore."

## Using the Left Brain (Problem Solving)

Chacha Chaudhary explained, "If you are facing a problem, like a tough math question or any life trouble, you should use your left brain. This means thinking logically, understanding the information well, and analysing it to find a solution."

Chhotu asked, "But Chacha ji, what if we are feeling scared?"

Chacha Chaudhary smiled and said, "To overcome fear, we need to take help from the right brain."

## Using the Right Brain (Creativity and Visualization)

Chacha Chaudhary explained, "If you ever feel scared, use your imagination. The right brain is connected to your creativity and emotions. Whenever fear arises, close your eyes and imagine a beautiful place. For example, picture yourself walking in the mountains, sitting by a peaceful lake, or flying in the sky. This technique will calm your mind and eliminate the fear."

Sabu said, "Wow! I always use my right brain when I get angry. When I'm angry, I picture myself in a calm place."

## Brain Exercise

Chacha Chaudhary shared another fun tip. He said, "If you want to strengthen both parts of your brain together, try some special brain exercises. For example, play crossword puzzles or Sudoku, draw pictures, or listen to music. This will keep your brain balanced and healthy."

Pinki asked eagerly, "Chacha ji, will this also reduce stress?"

Chacha Chaudhary nodded and said, "Absolutely! Stress arises when there is imbalance in the brain. If you keep both parts of your brain strong, not only will your creativity increase, but your logical thinking will also become sharper, and stress will disappear."

### Meditation and Deep Breathing

Chacha Chaudhary shared the last and simplest technique: "If you suddenly feel stressed, take a few deep breaths and meditate. This method will quickly calm your mind and balance both parts of your brain. It will bring mental peace, and the fear will disappear."

After a few days of following the techniques Chacha Chaudhary shared, all the villagers were able to overcome their stress and fear. They brought balance into their lives and started facing every challenge with laughter and ease.

Sabu said, "Now, whenever I get stuck in a problem, I use my left brain to find a solution, and if I feel scared, I lose myself in the creativity of my right brain. Truly, the game of the brain is amazing!"

Chacha Chaudhary laughed and said, "Remember, to drive away stress and fear in life, learn to use your mind correctly. Your mind is your greatest companion, and when you use both parts of it properly, no difficulty can scare you."

## Topic 1.2 - Chacha Chaudhary and Mind-Body Synchronization

One day, Chacha Chaudhary, Sabu, and Chhotu were sitting in the courtyard of Chacha's house, enjoying a cup of tea. Suddenly, Chhotu curiously asked, "Chacha ji, I've heard that it's very important to have synchronization between the mind and the body. But how does this synchronization work?"

Chacha Chaudhary smiled and replied, "Chhotu, this is a very important question. Mind-body synchronization, as it is called in English, is one of the greatest powers of our life. When our thoughts are clear and creative, and the body works in that direction, we can achieve something amazing."

Chacha Ji adjusted his cap and said, "Plato, the great Greek philosopher, used to say, 'The first and greatest victory is to conquer yourself.' This means that when we control our mind and body, we can face any challenge. The proper synchronization of the mind's power and the body's actions helps us achieve any goal."

Chhotu asked, "Chacha ji, is there an example that can help us understand this better?"

Chacha Chaudhary explained, "Of course! Take the example of Thomas Edison. When he dreamed of creating the electric bulb, he had thoughts and imagination in his mind. But if his hands and body hadn't worked on those thoughts, would he have been able to make the bulb? That's the power of synchronization. The mind thinks, but the body turns those thoughts into reality."

Sabu nodded and said, "So, if we want to create something new or achieve something big, both our mind and body need to work together?"

Chacha Ji smiled and replied, "Absolutely! Leonardo da Vinci, the great painter and inventor, used to say, 'Where the spirit does not work with the hand, there is no art.' This means that when our mind and body don't work together, creativity becomes impossible."

Chhotu asked again, "So, Chacha Ji, if someone's mind and body don't work together, they can't achieve anything big?"

Chacha Chaudhary said seriously, “Look, Chhotu, this is also taught in Buddhism. Buddha said, ‘The mind is everything. What you think, you become.’ This means that if we bring negative thoughts into our mind, our body will also work in accordance with those thoughts. But if we keep positive, creative, and energetic thoughts in our mind, our body will function the same way. That is true synchronization.”

Sabu asked, “So, how can we achieve this synchronization?”

Chacha Chaudhary explained, “To do this, we must first keep our mind calm. Regular meditation and yoga are important. Meditation not only calms the mind but also synchronizes the body. When the mind is clear, the body works without any interruptions. You’ve probably heard the saying, ‘A sound mind in a sound body.’ This saying reflects the idea that a healthy mind is the key to synchronizing with a healthy body.”

Chhotu asked again, “So when we think of something, and our body works accordingly, is that the right synchronization?”

Chacha Chaudhary nodded, “Exactly. Take another example from Albert Einstein. His mind was deeply immersed in the theory of relativity. But if his body hadn’t worked in that direction, perhaps he would never have been able to prove his ideas scientifically. This synchronization made him great.”

Chhotu smiled and said, “Now I understand, Chacha Ji! When we think positively and make our body work accordingly, only then can we achieve something big.”

Chacha Chaudhary picked up a small stone and threw it into the air, saying, “Remember, Chhotu, when the mind and body are in sync, creativity and imagination reach their peak. This is why history’s greatest inventions and creations happened when both thought and action were in harmony.”

Sabu finally said, "So this is true knowledge – aligning our thoughts and body."

Chacha Chaudhary laughed and replied, "Absolutely right! This is 'mind-body synchronization.' When this alignment happens, no dream is impossible in life."

## Topic 1.3 - Normal Brain vs Chacha Chaudhary's Brain – T Analysis

The brain is an amazing power that, when used in the right direction at the right time, can do incredible things. But can everyone's brain be as fast and sharp as Chacha Chaudhary's? We all know that Chacha Chaudhary's brain works faster than a computer. But have you ever wondered what the difference is between his brain and our normal brain?

Chacha Chaudhary's brain can find solutions to any problem in an instant, while a normal brain takes time to think, understand, and make decisions. Chacha Chaudhary's thinking has a deep combination of clarity and creativity, which sets him apart from others. In contrast, a normal brain struggles with doubts and obstacles.

Chacha Chaudhary's mind is always focused on solving problems, while a normal brain sometimes slows down by getting tangled in thoughts. Chacha Chaudhary's brain is not just fast, but also has an extraordinary ability to analyse and imagine. This is why he can quickly find solutions to even the toughest problems.

This analysis helps us understand why Chacha Chaudhary's brain is so special. His brain works not just because of information and experience, but because of a perfect combination of mental clarity, thinking ability, and creativity.

Here is the tabular form of the provided content in easy and readable English:

| | **Normal Brain** | **Chacha Chaudhary's Brain** |
|---|---|---|
| Visualization | The normal brain sees and thinks about situations in a simple way. | Chacha Chaudhary's brain can imagine anything and find a solution to the problem. |
| Association | The normal brain takes time to connect information and often gets distracted. | In Chacha Chaudhary's brain, all information is linked, which helps him understand everything correctly. |
| Positive Thinking | The normal brain often gets caught in negativity and struggles with problems. | Chacha Chaudhary always maintains a positive mindset and sees opportunities in every problem. |
| Innovation | The normal brain relies on old methods. | Chacha Chaudhary finds solutions with new and revolutionary ideas for every problem. |
| Focus | The normal brain easily gets distracted and cannot focus for long periods. | Chacha Chaudhary's focus stays fully intact, no matter how complex the situation. |
| Interest and Concentration | The normal brain works without interest, causing concentration to quickly fade. | Chacha Chaudhary takes deep interest in any problem and maintains his concentration. |

❒

CONCENTRATION
'Concentration is never weak or strong'
Interest and Concentration are best friends

Have we ever thought of
Students' Confusions???
Short Answers????
How to recall quickly
and avoid mistakes
in examinations?
How to overcome
examination
phobia??
K2SO4 AL2(SO4)3 24H2O ????
How to create
interest in
Studies ?
Long theory????
MCQ????
C3H7COOCH3 → Methyl Butyrate

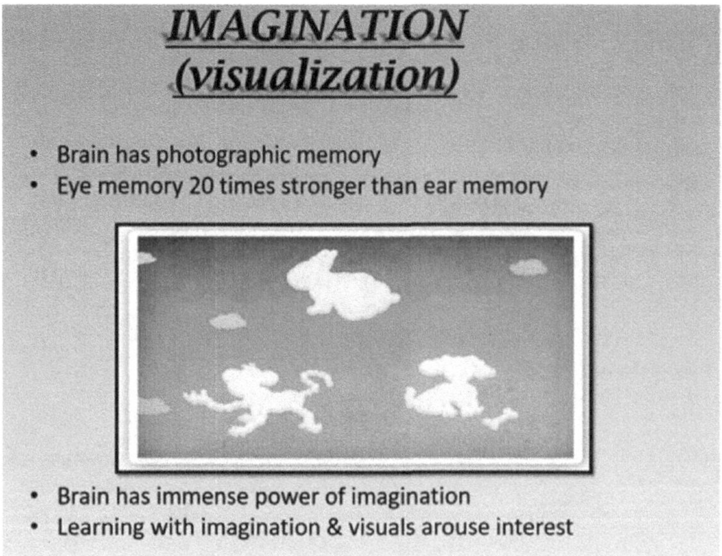
IMAGINATION
(visualization)
• Brain has photographic memory
• Eye memory 20 times stronger than ear memory
• Brain has immense power of imagination
• Learning with imagination & visuals arouse interest

*Chapter 2*

# What to Learn from Chacha Chaudhary's Life? What Should Children, Parents, and Teachers Learn?

Learning and teaching are lifelong processes. Whenever someone learns from another, it is often from their ideal person, a scholar, or a great personality. But when it comes to learning from Chacha Chaudhary's life, a unique excitement fills the mind.

This unusual and extraordinary comic character, who became a part of everyone's life through stories, entertained and resolved problems with his sharp mind and experiences. At times, he seemed like a teacher, at other times like a parent, and sometimes even like a friend to children.

When I was young, probably in fourth or fifth grade, I first got my hands on a Chacha Chaudhary comic. The colourful pages, the clever and insightful stories of Chacha Chaudhary, and the strength of Sabu captivated me so much that I started finding excuses to buy a new comic every week.

The stories of Chacha Chaudhary had a special charm. Not only were they fun, but they also carried a lesson at the end of every tale. He became my favourite character—so simple, yet so extraordinary. Every page of his stories transported me to a new world.

Chacha Chaudhary's famous line, *"Chacha Chaudhary's brain works faster than a computer,"* still resonates in my mind. It wasn't just a humorous statement but a reminder that with the right mindset and intelligence, every problem has a solution.

As a child, I considered these stories mere entertainment. But now, as I face the challenges of life, I realize Chacha Chaudhary was more than just a comic character. His tales held profound life lessons that we can apply in our daily lives.

I recall that no matter how big a problem was, Chacha Chaudhary never panicked. He always had a solution, often stemming from his sharp mind and vast experience. He taught us that every challenge in life has a resolution; we just need the right perspective and patience to find it.

Whether meant for children or adults, his stories always carried a message: to face problems with calmness and wisdom.

Now, when I look at these stories from the perspective of parents and teachers, I realize that Chacha Chaudhary's tales were not just about entertainment for children but also imparted important life lessons. For instance, children were taught never to make decisions in anger and to remain patient in difficult situations. I recall how, whenever I struggled in an exam or couldn't solve a question, the image of Chacha Chaudhary would come to mind. I'd wonder how he would tackle the problem. This would encourage me to think calmly and analytically.

Over time, I began to understand the value of patience and reasoning. Chacha Chaudhary's stories fostered a mindset in me that continues to help me face life's challenges with a calm and composed approach.

Now, when I look at these stories from the perspective of parents and teachers, I realize that Chacha Chaudhary's tales were not just about entertainment for children but also imparted important life lessons. For instance, children were taught never to make decisions in anger and to remain patient in difficult situations.

I recall how, whenever I struggled in an exam or couldn't solve a question, the image of Chacha Chaudhary would come to mind. I'd wonder how he would tackle the problem. This would encourage me to think calmly and analytically.

Over time, I began to understand the value of patience and reasoning. Chacha Chaudhary's stories fostered a mindset in me that continues to help me face life's challenges with a calm and composed approach.

Chacha Chaudhary always remained calm, whether facing a formidable villain like Raka or dealing with any other problem. This trait teaches children that they should never give up and must confront challenges head-on, no matter how big they seem.

Despite leading such a simple life, Chacha Chaudhary accomplished extraordinary feats. Parents, too, can learn the importance of teaching their children the value of simplicity and humility. This quality was clearly evident in Chacha Chaudhary's life—he never showed off but instead used his knowledge and experience to help others.

For parents, this is a vital lesson: they should instil in their children the significance of simplicity and helping others, guiding them to move in the right direction in life.

Chacha Chaudhary's stories also offer valuable lessons for teachers. His problem-solving skills demonstrate that every issue can have more than one solution—it simply requires the right perspective. Teachers can adopt this approach to guide their students effectively in all situations.

Chacha Chaudhary never considered anyone inferior or weak; he always treated everyone with equal respect. Teachers should also understand that every student is unique and must be given the opportunity to grow at their own pace.

Knowledge is not limited to books alone; teaching how to apply it in practical life is equally important.

Today, when I think about it, I realize that Chacha Chaudhary's stories not only filled my childhood with laughter and fun but also taught me many invaluable lessons about life.

Their simplicity, humility, and never-give-up attitude continue to inspire me even today. Perhaps that's why Chacha Chaudhary is not just a fictional character but one of the most important role models in my life. I hope that future generations also learn to approach life with the wisdom, simplicity, and patience exemplified by Chacha Chaudhary.

## Topic 2.1 - Chacha Chaudhary's Science: The Secrets of Interest and Concentration

It was summer vacation, and Pinki, Rakesh, and Sabu were sitting at Chacha Chaudhary's house. Pinki couldn't focus on her studies. Rakesh was holding a book, but his eyes were glued to the TV. Sabu was sitting in a corner, relaxing and admiring his muscles.

Pinki took a deep breath and said, "Chacha Ji, I don't understand how people concentrate on studying. Whenever I sit down to study, my mind wanders somewhere else.

Rakesh also agreed, "Yes, Chacha Ji, whenever I open my books, I get bored within minutes. But when it comes to the TV or my mobile, I can concentrate easily."

Chacha Chaudhary smiled and said, "The solution to both of your problems is interest. When you are interested in something, concentration comes naturally. Interest and concentration are the best friends."

Rakesh eagerly asked, "Chacha Ji, how can you say that interest and concentration are friends?"

Chacha Chaudhary explained in his unique way, "Look, my child, if you are interested in something, you don't need to force yourself to concentrate. For example, when you're watching an exciting movie, your attention is completely on the film, no matter how much noise is around. Interest brings concentration along with it."

Sabu also added, "Exactly! When I'm wrestling, I don't think about anything else. My full concentration is only on the match because I enjoy it."

Pinki asked, "But Chacha Ji, if we don't always have peace around us, how can we concentrate?"

Chacha Ji laughed and said, "If you are interested in what you're doing, you won't need peace. Just like when you're watching your favourite cartoons or playing games, you don't need to search for peace, because your attention naturally focuses on that thing."

## "How to make studying fun?"

Rakesh hesitated and asked, "Chacha Ji, so can we make studying interesting in a way that our attention naturally focuses on it?"

Chacha Chaudhary nodded and said, "Absolutely! To make studying fun, we need to use some special techniques. I will teach you techniques like association and imagination, which will turn your studies into a game. For example, if you need to remember a difficult word or date, link it with a fun story or image. When things become enjoyable, your attention will automatically follow."

Chacha Chaudhary said, "Remember, kids! Whenever you face difficulty in focusing, first try to find interest in that task.

If there is no interest, and you want to make studying fun, then use techniques like the association principle, also known as the companion principle. If a topic is hard to remember, associate it with another topic or an image that will help you recall it. Just like when you watch a movie, you never forget the story. Similarly, if you create pictures in your studies, it will become easier to remember."

Pinki excitedly said, "This will be so much fun, Chacha Ji! I will even look at my math problems like a game!"

Pinki and Rakesh listened carefully to Chacha Chaudhary's words and decided in their hearts that they would make their studies interesting. They realized that interest and concentration are truly the best of friends, and when these two are together, nothing feels difficult.

## Topic 2.2 - Chacha Chaudhary's Master Plan: Finish the Syllabus on Time and Top the Exam

One day, Chacha Chaudhary was sitting at home with his dear friend, Vinod Sharma, when Pinki and Rakesh came to them. The worry was clearly visible on their faces. Pinki said, "Chacha Ji, our exams are approaching, and we don't know how to finish the entire syllabus and revise properly. We keep studying again and again, but nothing seems to stay in our memory."

Rakesh also expressed his concern, "Yes, Chacha Ji, we do study, but whenever we sit down to revise, everything starts to feel boring. How will we do well in the revision?"

Chacha Chaudhary smiled and said, "The solution to your problem is very simple, and today I will get it solved by my dear friend, who is an excellent brain science trainer. He has in-depth knowledge of memory techniques (mnemonics) that make studying easier."

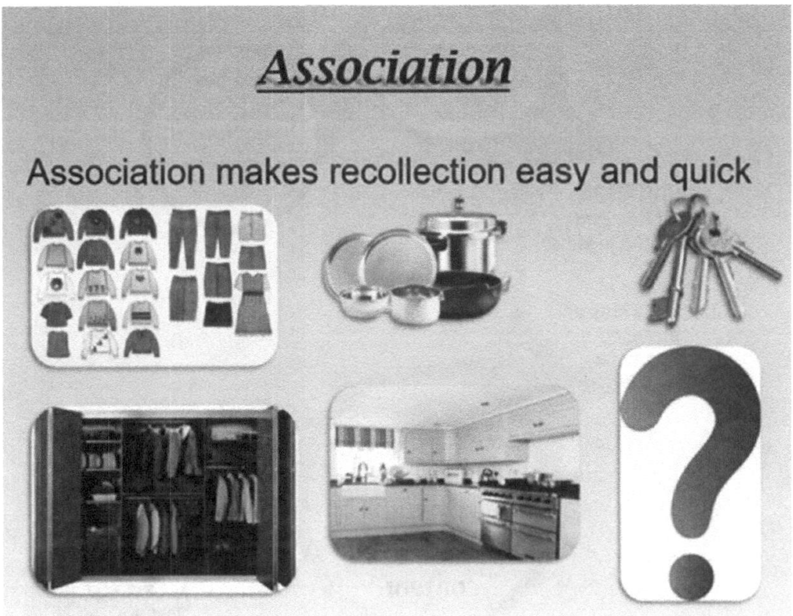
Association
Association makes recollection easy and quick

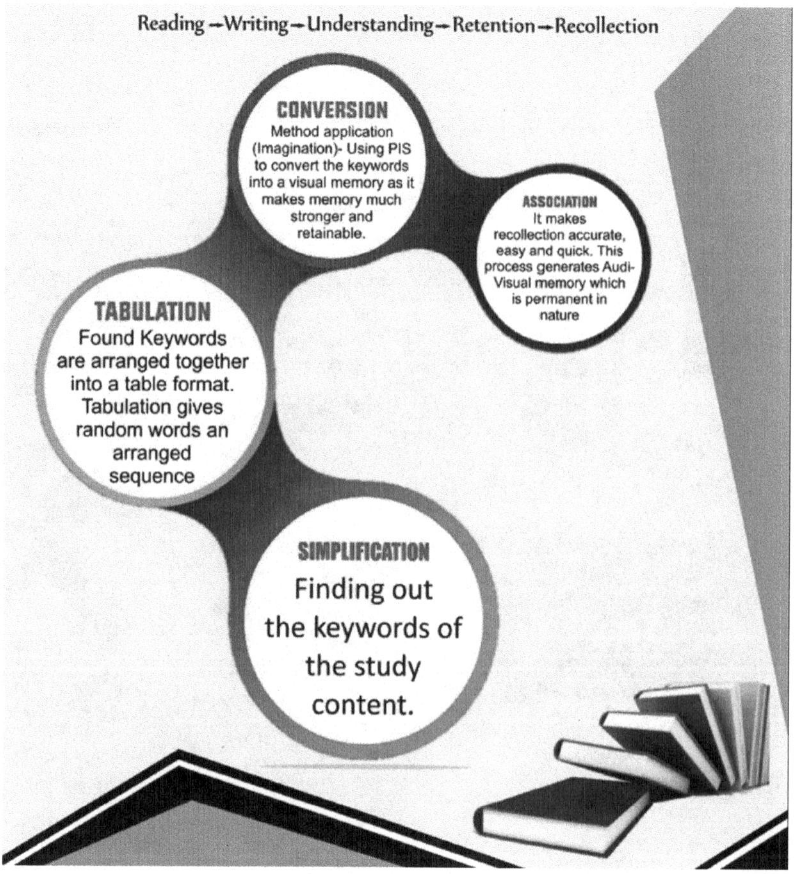

Reading → Writing → Understanding → Retention → Recollection
CONVERSION
Method application (Imagination)- Using PIS to convert the keywords into a visual memory as it makes memory much stronger and retainable.
ASSOCIATION
It makes recollection accurate, easy and quick. This process generates Audi-Visual memory which is permanent in nature
TABULATION
Found Keywords are arranged together into a table format. Tabulation gives random words an arranged sequence
SIMPLIFICATION
Finding out the keywords of the study content.

Vinod Sharma said, "Children, before you understand what revision really means, you must know its true purpose." He explained, "You all might think that simply reading the same material repeatedly is revision, but that's not the case. The term 'vision' means 'to see,' and 'revision' means 'to see again.' For example, when you watch a movie, that's called 'vision,' and when you watch the same movie again, it's called 'revision.'"

Pinki looked surprised and asked, "So, does studying mean watching a movie?"

Vinod smiled and replied, "Repeating the same thing can be boring, but if you can turn your lessons into visual scenes, studying becomes enjoyable. Just like you watch movies again and have fun, if you turn your lessons into images or stories, understanding them becomes easier and more interesting."

## The Art of Revision

Chacha Chaudhary said, "You need to make revision like watching something again instead of just reading it again. If you transform your studies into pictures or maps and mentally visualize them, they will always be remembered. When you watch movies repeatedly, you always notice something new—that's the real benefit of revision. For example, instead of memorizing a historical event, you can live its story in your imagination. This way, the event will never be forgotten."

Sabu, who had been quietly listening until now, said, "So, Chacha, does this mean we have to transform our studies into pictures and stories in our minds?"

Chacha nodded and said, "Exactly, Sabu! And Vinod added that you should transform the subject of your studies into visuals and stories in your mind. For example, if you need to remember a royal battle, create an imaginary movie of it and watch it in your mind. Doing this will make your revision fun."

Now, Rakesh asked, "But Chacha Ji, how can we complete the syllabus on time? We have very little time."

Chacha Chowdhury replied, "Let me tell you about the syllabus.

"To complete the syllabus on time, the first thing you need is a plan. Just like you divide a big task into smaller parts, divide the syllabus into chunks and study it. Make a schedule to study specific subjects every day and progress according to that."

Pinki said cheerfully, "So, we have to study a little every day and make a plan?"

Chacha nodded in agreement and said, "For this, we need a special plan. First, make a list of subjects. Under each subject, write down the subtitles. Then, under each subtitle, write down the theory. After that, use the technique of simplification."

Chacha Chowdhury explained, "In this technique, you extract the key words from the full theory and write them in a table. Then, create associations between these key words, using your creativity and imagination. Finally, visualize it in your mind. This will not only make the syllabus easier, but it will also save your time."

Then, Chacha, making the children laugh, recited a poem:

*"Do your tasks with joy and ease,*
*Focus on your studies, if you please.*
*Make stories, add pictures bright,*
*Revision will make your learning light."*

Finally, Chacha Chowdhury said, "If you study in a creative way and divide the syllabus into small parts, not only will you be able to finish on time, but revision will also become fun. Remember, revision means reviewing, so adopt the right way to review and make your studies as enjoyable as a movie!"

The children happily said, "Thank you, Chacha Ji! Thank you, Vinod Sir! Now we won't see studies as a burden, but will approach them in a fun way!"

## Topic 2.3 - The Union of Students, Teachers, and Parents

One day, Chacha Chaudhary and his friend Vinod Sharma were relaxing at home. Suddenly, Pinki and Rakesh came running to them, their faces showing clear concern.

Pinki said, "Chacha Ji, our teachers and parents have so many expectations from us. We don't know how to meet them."

Rakesh added, "Chacha Ji, sometimes it all feels so overwhelming. Are we doing something wrong?"

Chacha Chaudhary smiled warmly and said, "Children, what you're feeling is normal. But it's important to understand the vital roles that your teachers, parents, and you yourself play in your life. These three are incomplete without each other."

Vinod Sharma, an expert in brain science, nodded in agreement and said, "Children, if we understand the contributions of all three—students, teachers, and parents—in the right way, achieving our goals becomes much easier. Let Chacha Ji and me explain this to you in detail."

### 1. Teachers - The Guiding Light

Chacha Chaudhary said, "Teachers don't just teach lessons from textbooks; they guide you in every aspect of life. They possess the knowledge and experience to show you the right path. Teachers are like lamps that dispel darkness and illuminate the road ahead for you."

"Think about it—without your teachers, how would you solve complex math problems? Or understand the fascinating facts of science? A teacher's role is not just to help you score marks in exams but also to help you grasp the essence of life."

### *Important Message:*

*"Teachers inspire you to walk in the right direction. Respect their words and listen to them attentively, as it will brighten your future. Follow the guidance they provide, for it will help you tackle every challenge in life."*

Sanskrit Shloka:

गुरुर्ब्रह्मा गुरुर्विष्णुः गुरुर्देवो महेश्वरः।
गुरुः साक्षात् परं ब्रह्म तस्मै श्रीगुरुवे नमः।।

*(The Guru is Brahma, the Guru is Vishnu, the Guru is Lord Maheshwara. The Guru is indeed the Supreme Absolute. Salutations to that revered Guru.)*

Pinki and Rakesh listened intently and thought, "Our teachers are truly the guides of our lives. We must pay attention to their words."

---

## 2. Parents - Your Foundation

Chacha Chaudhary then explained the importance of parents, saying,

"Your parents are your roots. Just as the roots of a tree provide strength and nourishment, your parents form the foundation of your life. They take care of all your needs, be they physical or mental.

"You must have noticed that when you fall ill, who worries the most? When you're about to make an important decision in life, who advises you? It's your parents who stand by you through thick and thin, in your good times and bad."

---

### *Important Message:*

*"Without parents, the foundation of life becomes weak. Their love and discipline help you walk the right path in life. Following their advice will make you stronger. They not only fulfil your needs but also shape your character and thinking."*

Rakesh nodded and said, "Chacha Ji, now we understand how much our parents do for us. We must always listen to their advice."

## 3. Children - The Hope of the Future

Chacha Chaudhary said,

"Children, you are the future of society. As you progress, society will also move forward. There are immense possibilities hidden within you, and it is your duty to recognize and use them wisely.

"When you are young, you may not know what you should do. But as you grow, your teachers and parents guide you in the right direction. Now, it is your responsibility to believe in yourself and learn from your mistakes."

### *Important Message:*

*"Children, it is essential to believe in yourself. Understand your responsibilities and work towards building your future. While following the advice of your parents and teachers, make use of your creativity and intelligence."*

## 4. The role of everyone

"Finally, Chacha Chaudhary explained, 'In life, the roles of teachers, parents, and children are interconnected. Just like the roots, trunk, and leaves of a tree depend on each other, these three are essential for your success.'

## Conclusion of the Story:

*The purpose of this story is to help children understand the importance of teachers, parents, and their own role in their lives. Together, these three contribute to making life successful, and with harmony, any obstacle can be overcome."*

## Topic 2.4 - The Four Dimensions of Education – Chacha Chaudhary's Unique Classroom

Chacha Chaudhary was enjoying tea with his wife, Bini, while reading the newspaper. Suddenly, there was a loud knock on the door. When the door opened, Ballu Pahalwan, who was always looking for new ways to challenge Chacha Chaudhary, entered. This time, there was a mischievous smile on his face, but it was clear he was ready for a mental challenge.

**Raka:** "Chacha Chaudhary, you've talked a lot about your strength, but can you tell me what the true meaning of education is? Why are children so caught up in studies these days?"

Chacha Chaudhary smiled and said, "Ballu, that's quite an interesting question. But how did this thought come to your mind? Since when did you start developing an interest in education?"

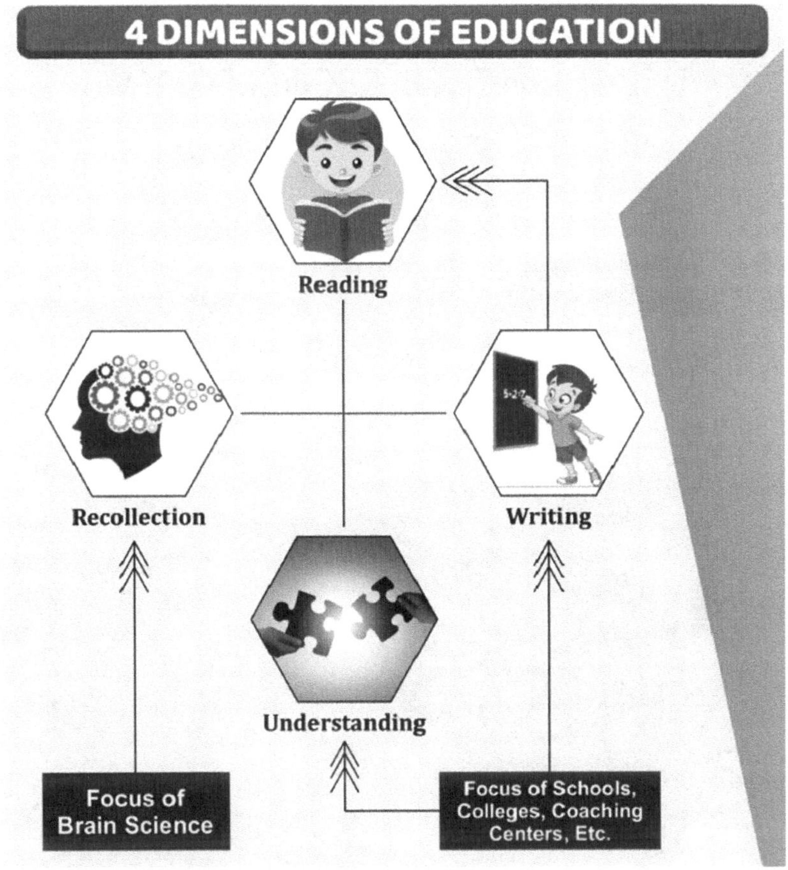
4 DIMENSIONS OF EDUCATION
Reading
Recollection
Writing
Understanding
Focus of Brain Science
Focus of Schools, Colleges, Coaching Centers, Etc.

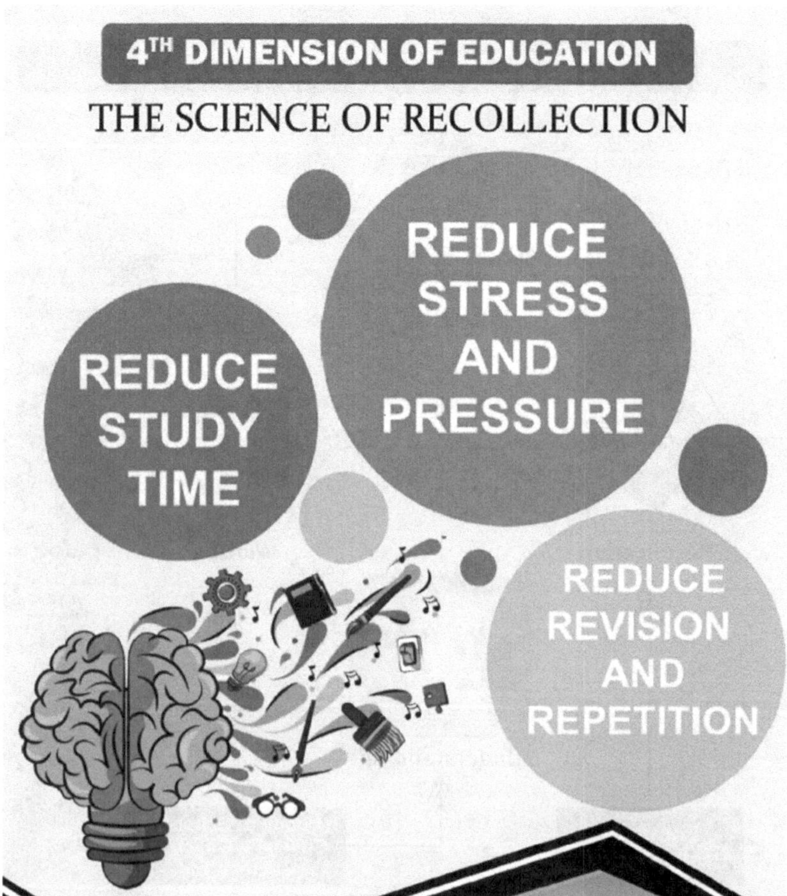
4TH DIMENSION OF EDUCATION
THE SCIENCE OF RECOLLECTION
REDUCE STUDY TIME
REDUCE STRESS AND PRESSURE
REDUCE REVISION AND REPETITION

"Ballu Pahalwan, scratching his head a little shyly, said, 'Well, some guests came to my house, and I overheard them talking about it. So, I thought of coming to you to learn more."

Chacha smiled and said, "If that's the case, sit down and listen carefully. Education is based on four main dimensions:

1. **Cognizance** (Knowing),
2. **Kinesthesis** (Action),
3. **Comprehension** (Understanding), and
4. **Recollection** (Remembering).

Once these four dimensions are understood, studying will no longer feel like a burden or a puzzle."

Bini, who was sitting nearby, grew curious and said, "Please explain to me as well how these four dimensions work!"

## The First Dimension – Cognizance (Knowing):

Chacha Chaudhary began explaining, "The first dimension is 'Knowing.' Knowing means acquiring information. When we read something new, like a newspaper, a book, or notes, our brain stores that new information. For example, I just read in the newspaper that heavy rains have caused floods in some places. This information is now registered in my mind. This process is what we call 'Knowing.'"

He gave an example to clarify, "When children learn a new math formula for the first time, they only hear or read it. At this stage, their brain is simply storing the information. But is that enough?"

Ballu Pahalwan nodded his head, "No, Chacha ji, that's why kids tend to forget those formulas repeatedly."

Chacha replied, "Exactly, Ballu! Merely knowing is not enough."

### The Second Dimension – Kinesthesis (Action):

Chacha Chaudhary continued, "Now comes the second dimension – Kinesthesis, which means learning through the use of hands and body. When a child writes a math formula on paper, their muscles become connected with the learning process."

Chacha Chaudhary continued, "'Action' or 'Kinesthesis', refers to the process of doing things. For example, when children write '2×3' on paper, their hands and brain work together. This process makes learning permanent."

He gave another example, "If you've learned to ride a bicycle, initially, it may be difficult to understand. But as you practice riding the bicycle repeatedly, your body eventually memorizes it. This is the action-based learning."

Bini said, "So, it means that the things we do retain in our memory for a longer time."

Chacha Chaudhary nodded and said, "Exactly right. Now, let's move on to the dimension of understanding."

### The Third Dimension – Comprehension (Understanding):

Chacha Chaudhary explained, "'Understanding' is the process where we connect what we've read or done to our real life. When a child understands that '2×3' means two groups with three objects each, they grasp the meaning of multiplication."

Bini asked, "What if I just want to memorize?"

Chacha Chaudhary smiled and replied, "Memorization may be temporary. But if you understand something, it stays with you for life. For example, if a child understands how a math concept will be useful in real life, like for counting money or calculating time, they will never forget it."

### The Fourth Dimension – Recollection (Memory):

Now, Chacha Chaudhary explained the final dimension, "Lastly, we have 'Recollection', which means reviewing what we have learned (recollection). After studying, we need to revise the information periodically. When we recall what we have read, done, and understood, it becomes solidified in our memory." He continued, "It is this Recollection that helps us write during exams. But recollection will only happen if the information is permanently stored in our minds. To make it permanent, imagination and visualization play a significant role." He gave an example, "When a child repeats a lesson over and over again, or takes a quiz on a subject, their brain stores the information for a long time. For instance, after watching a movie, we remember its story because it was repeated multiple times."

Similarly, if we approach our studies like a movie—reading and understanding them in-depth—they will stay with us permanently. And as they say, 'What is seen and heard often in life stays in memory.'

Ballu Pahalwan was now a bit surprised. "So, does that mean in studies, it's not just about rote memorization, but we should learn by understanding these four dimensions?"

Chacha Chaudhary replied, "Exactly! Now, imagine if both teachers and students focus on these four dimensions, studying will not only become easier but also more interesting."

If teachers also ensure that children understand what they read and do, and connect it to life, and periodically make them review, quizzes, tests, and discussions will strengthen this process.

Ballu Pahalwan finally accepted that Chacha Chaudhary's ideas about education were correct. Nodding his head, he said, "Chacha, arguing with you is pointless. Now, I will also study using these four dimensions, so I too can have a sharp mind like yours."

Chacha Chaudhary, laughing, said, "Not just a sharp mind, but you will also become someone who understands the true meaning of education."

Ha ha ha ha!

## Topic 2.5 - Chacha Chaudhary's Tips: Habits of Successful Students

One day, Pinki, Raka, and Sabu were sitting at Chacha Chaudhary's house, having fun. Suddenly, Pinki's mother called her from home and said, "The whole day has passed, and there's no concern about studying, eating, or even the upcoming exams." Pinki replied, "I'll come in a little while. Anyway, I'm not hungry, and no matter how much I study, my marks will still be low."

Pinki said, "Chacha Ji, we work really hard, but it feels like there's never enough time and the burden of studies is too much. We can't focus on studying properly, and sometimes we can't even sleep well. What should we do?" Then, Pinki's mother added, "Yes, Chacha Ji, please tell us something. If the kids think like this, how will they study and move forward?"

## Chacha Chaudhary's Tips: Habits of Successful Students

Chacha Chaudhary, with his famous smile, said, "First of all, it's important to understand what habits are. If we have knowledge and apply it in our life, it becomes a habit. For example, by practicing time management and good habits, you can succeed not only in exams but also in life. I will tell you about some habits that will make your studies more effective."

## Positive Thinking and Time Management

Chacha Chaudhary first explained, "The most important thing in studies is positive thinking. When you believe that you can do it, only then success will come. Leave behind negativity and always maintain a positive mindset."

Chacha Chaudhary explained about time management, saying, "You need to set a specific time for studying every day. Using time effectively is the key. If you plan properly, you will have time for studying as well as for rest and other activities."

## Studying in Intervals and Good Sleep

Chacha Chaudhary further explained, "It is important to study in intervals. Studying continuously for long hours tires the brain. Therefore, after every one hour of studying, take a 10–15-minute break. This will refresh your mind and make studying more effective."

Then, he emphasized, "And yes, make sure to pay attention to good sleep. It is also important to get enough sleep along with studying. With eight hours of sleep at night, your brain functions better and helps in retaining information."

## Innovation and Healthy Food

"You should always use innovation in your studies," Chacha Chaudhary explained. "If you think in new ways, like using pictures, stories, or imagination, even difficult things will be easier to remember. Try new techniques every time; it will make studying more interesting."

Sabu asked, "Chacha, does food also make a difference in studying?"

Chacha Chaudhary smiled and replied, "Absolutely! Healthy and nutritious food energizes the brain. Eat fresh fruits, vegetables, and dry fruits. Minimize fried or junk food so that both your body and mind stay active."

## Meditation and Exercise

Chacha Chaudhary said, "Practice meditation and exercise every day. Meditation brings peace to the mind and helps you stay focused. Exercise keeps the body fit, and you feel refreshed."

## Exam Planning and Concentration

"Planning for exams is very important," Chacha Chaudhary advised. "Before exams, make a schedule for the subjects you need to study. Divide your time and stick to it. This way, you will finish the entire syllabus on time."

Then Chacha Ji discussed another important habit, "Whenever you study, focus on one thing at a time. If your concentration wanders, you won't remember anything. Stay away from distractions like mobile phones and TV, and focus only on one thing."

Pinki, Rakesh, and Sabu listened carefully to all of Chacha Chaudhary's words. Pinki, feeling happy, said, "Chacha Ji, now we will adopt the habits you've shared and make our studies even better."

Chacha Chaudhary, smiling, replied, "Remember, studying is not just about hard work, but it can also be easier with the right habits and plans. And our right habits give us success not only in exams but in life as well."

---

## Topic 2.6 - Chacha Chaudhary and the Five Pillars of Happiness

One day, Chacha Chaudhary, his wife Bini, Sabu, and Chhotu were sitting in the garden of their house. The weather was pleasant, and everyone was enjoying their tea.

Then Bini said, "Chaudhary Ji, I feel that true happiness is not just about earning money. True happiness lies in many things."

Chacha Chaudhary smiled and said, "Absolutely right, Bini. Happiness has many pillars."

Sabu, who was quietly sipping his tea, said, "Chacha ji, I'm also curious to know more."

Chacha Chaudhary explained, "There are five pillars of happiness:

i. Health,
ii. Wealth,
iii. Wisdom,
iv. Spirituality, and
v. Relationships.

Life is incomplete without these five."

## 1. Health (स्वास्थ्य)

Chacha Chaudhary explained the first pillar: "Health is the most important. There is an old saying, 'The first wealth is health.' If the body is healthy, you can do anything."

Chhotu, jokingly, said, "Chacha Ji, if I keep eating sweets every day, will I stay healthy?"

Chacha Ji, laughing, replied, "Absolutely not! Sweets might make your stomach happy, but they won't give strength to your body. Only good food, exercise, and enough sleep can keep you healthy. Look at Sabu; he exercises every day, and that's why he is always strong."

Sabu, showing his muscles, said, "Yes, I enjoy exercising every day. That's the secret of my strength."

## 2. Wealth (धन)

Chacha Chaudhary then spoke about wealth: "Wealth is important, but happiness cannot be bought with money alone. As Bini rightly said, wealth provides comfort, but true happiness comes when we spend it on the right things."

Bini added, "Yes, Choudhary Ji, money should not be wasted. It should be saved and used wisely."

Chhotu, mischievously, asked, "So, Chacha Ji, if I have a lot of money, will I be happy?"

Chacha Ji replied, "If you use money in the right way—helping those in need, securing your family, and planning for the future—you will be happy. Just hoarding it won't bring happiness."

## 3. Wisdom (ज्ञान)

Chacha Chaudhary emphasized the importance of wisdom: "The third pillar is wisdom. A wise person can make the right decisions and lead their life in the right direction. Wisdom is not just found in books, but also in our experiences and life lessons."

Sabu, surprised, asked, "Chacha, you once said that whenever you face a problem, you don't refer to books but use your experiences instead."

Chacha Ji nodded and replied, "Exactly! The true knowledge of life is hidden in our experiences. The more you learn, the easier it becomes to face life's challenges."

Bini, laughing, added, "That's why Choudhary Ji is always reading books!"

## 4. Spirituality (आध्यात्मिक)

Chacha Chaudhary explained the fourth pillar: "Spirituality is the path to inner peace and true happiness. Spirituality helps us realize that we live not only for material happiness but also for spiritual fulfilment."

Sabu asked, "Chacha, what does spirituality mean?"

Chacha Ji explained, "Spirituality means the peace of the soul, meditation, and the art of looking within. As the Bhagavad Gita says, *'Yoga: karmasu kaushalam'*—through meditation and yoga, you can achieve skill in every task."

Bini added, "Chaudhary Ji, you practice meditation every day, that's why you always stay peaceful."

## 5. Relationships (रिश्ते)

Finally, Chacha Chaudhary spoke about relationships: "The fifth and strongest pillar of happiness is relationships. Good relationships bring love, support, and companionship in life. The bonds with family, friends, and society provide us with mental and emotional strength."

Chhotu asked, "But Chacha Ji, sometimes we have fights with friends or relatives. What should we do then?"

Chacha Ji smiled and said, "Relationships require patience and understanding. Fights are common, but resolving them is the true art. Love and forgiveness strengthen relationships."

Bini nodded in agreement and said, "Chaudhary Ji is right. Relationships support us at every step of life."

In conclusion, Chacha Chaudhary said, "So, children, if you adopt these five pillars—health, wealth, wisdom, spirituality, and relationships—in your life, your life will always be happy."

Sabu, Bini, and Chhotu said together, "Thank you, Chacha Ji, for showing us the true meaning of happiness."

Chacha Chaudhary smiled and said, "Remember, to stay happy, you shouldn't rely on just one thing. The combination of these five pillars is the secret to true happiness."

With that, Chacha Chaudhary recited a four-line poem:

*With health, wealth, and wisdom in tow,*
*Spirituality makes life glow.*
*Relationships bring joy to the soul,*
*These five pillars make happiness whole.*

## Topic 2.7 - How to Achieve Holistic Success and Become an Ideal Personality

In this section, we talk about what holistic success means. We can motivate a person to become a champion, but the champion must make themselves that way. We can guide someone to develop a personality, but a great personality is something that comes from within. In other words, through training and practice, we can achieve holistic success, but to elevate a skill to a higher level, personal interest and individual effort are essential; passion is required.

What does holistic success mean? In our lives, there are many things. Many educated people remain unemployed, while others, with less education, achieve immense success. One common factor among all those who are successful at a high level is that they have a sense of holistic success within them. You can train someone to develop an ideal personality, but a great person will emerge through their own efforts.

Now, how does this happen? A car's tire has a number written on it that indicates how much air should be pumped into it. If we inflate the tire with less air than the number suggests, the car will wobble, and if we overinflate it, the car will still wobble. This number is there to maintain balance. The car will only run smoothly when its balance is maintained.

Similarly, in our bodies, important parameters such as blood pressure and heart rate have specific numbers that keep our body functioning well. These numbers represent balance, and this balance keeps our body healthy. This concept of excellence means that we need to know the balance in our lives. Practice makes a person excellent. The right habits become permanent habits, and the right habits make a person's personality exceptional.

## Meaning of Perfection:

Perfection means doing something in the most accepted and practical way. It demonstrates practical wisdom and efficiency. We become excellent in something through learning and studying. Perfection is the result of consistent effort. Now, how does perfection come? How does it develop in any skill? For example, how do we acquire skills like driving a car, cooking, or flying an airplane? As we mentioned before, practice makes a person excellent, and similarly, these skills come to us through continuous learning and practice, enabling us to achieve perfection.

When we practice something repeatedly, our brain creates a pattern, and we begin to achieve perfection in that skill. For example, we can become players, but someone like Sachin Tendulkar becomes a cricket legend through his own efforts. We can become actors, but Amitabh Bachchan is an icon in his own right. We can become singers, but Lata Mangeshkar is a legend in singing. We can become scientists, but Dr. A.P.J. Abdul Kalam became a renowned figure through his own efforts. In other words, we can inspire someone toward perfection, but only that person can actually attain mastery in a skill and move toward holistic success.

In the most successful people of the world, there are common qualities that make them exceptional and ideal personalities, and these can be seen in the pyramid given. It's not just about education; the skills listed in this pyramid are equally important in shaping an ideal personality. These skills are practical, social, self-related, and emotional, and balancing them is crucial. To build an ideal personality, we must continuously practice these skills over time.

An ideal person must have a balance of good skills along with moral values, discipline, proper etiquette, and good character. With all of these, a person becomes an ideal and capable individual.

## Meaning of Perfection:

Perfection means doing something in the most accepted and practical way. It demonstrates practical wisdom and efficiency. We become excellent in something through learning and studying. Perfection is the result of consistent effort. Now, how does perfection come? How does it develop in any skill? For example, how do we acquire skills like driving a car, cooking, or flying an airplane? As we mentioned before, practice makes a person excellent, and similarly, these skills come to us through continuous learning and practice, enabling us to achieve perfection.

When we practice something repeatedly, our brain creates a pattern, and we begin to achieve perfection in that skill. For example, we can become players, but someone like Sachin Tendulkar becomes a cricket legend through his own efforts. We can become actors, but Amitabh Bachchan is an icon in his own right. We can become singers, but Lata Mangeshkar is a legend in singing. We can become scientists, but Dr. A.P.J. Abdul Kalam became a renowned figure through his own efforts. In other words, we can inspire someone toward perfection, but only that person can actually attain mastery in a skill and move toward holistic success.

In the most successful people of the world, there are common qualities that make them exceptional and ideal personalities, and these can be seen in the pyramid given. It's not just about education; the skills listed in this pyramid are equally important in shaping an ideal personality. These skills are practical, social, self-related, and emotional, and balancing them is crucial. To build an ideal personality, we must continuously practice these skills over time.

An ideal person must have a balance of good skills along with moral values, discipline, proper etiquette, and good character. With all of these, a person not only becomes an ideal and capable individual but also a good human being, leading to holistic and complete success.

HOLISTIC SUCCESS

The purpose of education is to shape a person into a personality. The goal of practice is to make something easier. Chacha Chaudhary is an excellent blend of skill and personality. Sabu had great strength and was an exceptional person to some extent, but Chacha Chaudhary is a true and great source of inspiration and education. He trained Sabu, a giant from another planet, and guided him towards developing a great personality.

Overall development means instilling basic skills and knowledge in a person, so that an ideal personality can be reflected in them on a holistic level.

So, whether it's a teacher, a parent, or a child reading this, it is important to understand whether they possess these qualities or abilities within themselves to become an ideal personality. And if not, they should know how to acquire these abilities.

The given pyramid shows how, by acquiring these basic and essential abilities on time, you can achieve a holistic success and become an ideal personality.

## Topic 2.8 - How to Reduce the Time Spent on Preparation and Improve Exam Results: Chacha Chaudhary's Exam Science

One day, Chacha Ji and Chachi Ji were sitting together during their free time, chatting. Suddenly, Chacha Ji remembered something. He recalled how stressful it was when he used to study as a child. Now, when he sees other children studying, it all seems so much easier.

With this thought, a deep reflection began in Chacha Chaudhary's mind.

He started thinking about how to make children's studies and their student life easier, so they could enjoy their childhood.

Chacha Ji said to Chachi, "Do you know, to fight enemies like Raka, both mental and physical strength are required? Similarly, in children's lives, there are many 'Rakas' that are like their enemies.

"These include exams, tests, practical work, oral tests, making projects, and so on. Apart from these, there's also reading chapters, understanding them, writing them in a notebook, and then memorizing. Any task that children find difficult becomes like an enemy, just like Raka."

Chachi said, "The hardest task seems to be preparing for exams and remembering everything."

Chacha Ji then said, "Go and bring those children from the neighbourhood who are having trouble with their studies."

Chachi brought some children from the neighbourhood who were having difficulties with their studies.

Chacha Ji said to the children, "Children! Today I will talk about three topics that will make your studies easier.

First - Reducing repetition and revision. Second - Reducing study time. Third - Increasing result percentage.

Let's first talk about how to reduce repetition and revision in studies. First, let's understand why repetition and revision are done? And second, what are the benefits and drawbacks of it? Let's talk about it with a new topic.

## Purpose of repetition and revision

The purpose of repetition and revision is to ensure that whatever children study, it settles well in their minds and they don't face any issues in recalling it. This is an important process because it enhances the stability of the information and helps children remember what they've learned for a longer time.

Repetition has many benefits, but it also comes with some drawbacks. First, constantly repeating something can become boring, and children stop focusing on the content. Second, repeating anything consumes a lot of time, which disturbs other study sessions.

So, children, now what's the solution to this? The one and only solution is... using brain science techniques." "Brain science-based techniques like visualization, association (making connections), and mind mapping can help children reduce the need for repetition and revision. By using these techniques, children can grasp information more efficiently in less time.

Now, let's talk about the second topic."

## Reducing Study Time

The purpose of reducing study time is not for children to study less, but to help them learn more efficiently during their study time.

"Isn't that, right?" Chacha Ji said excitedly.

When a child uses brain science-based techniques correctly, they can not only remember information better but also reduce the time spent on studying.

Now, let's move on to the third topic, which is **Increasing Result Percentage.**

## Increasing Result Percentage

To improve results, it's important that children understand the concepts correctly and apply them on time. Instead of memorizing, understanding the concept is more important. Children can be encouraged through quizzes and positive reinforcement.

Chacha Ji said, "So children, now I think you must have understood how important brain science techniques are for scoring better marks in exams. When you use them, not only will you save time, but studying will also become fun and easy. Now, study smartly with hard work, and you will shine in your results!"

After listening to Chacha Ji's words, the children's faces lit up with new energy and confidence.

## Topic 2.9 - What Balances are Needed to Make a Family a Super Family? Chacha Chaudhary and the Secret of a Super Family: Balancing Work and Life

The mere mention of Chacha Chaudhary brings a smile to everyone's face. This sharp-minded man, whose brain works faster than a computer, always resolves even the most challenging problems with his intelligence and quick thinking. No matter how tough the situation, Chacha Chaudhary has a solution for every issue. His life is a perfect balance of timing and organization.

While his battles with villains are fascinating, today, we'll explore something equally intriguing—his secret to a **super family mantra.**

Chacha Chaudhary holds a secret that not only keeps his life sorted but also ensures that his family stays happy and united. That secret is **"balance,"** which we know as the balance between work and life.

Chacha Chaudhary understands that being engrossed only in work is not enough to fulfil responsibilities. Family and relationships must be given equal importance.

In today's world, the pressure of work is increasing for everyone. Children are busy with their school studies, parents are juggling between office and household responsibilities, and time seems to be insufficient in everyone's life. Everyone feels that 24 hours in a day are too little.

But Chacha Chaudhary doesn't believe that. For him, **proper time management** is the key that makes his family a super family.

### The Secret to Becoming a Super Family

Have you ever wondered why your family doesn't feel like a super family? **The Secret to a Super Family: Balance**

What makes Chacha Chaudhary's family so organized and

happy? The answer lies in one word: **Balance**. When we learn to balance our responsibilities, our lives and families transform into a super family. Chacha Chaudhary believes that a successful person is one who gives equal importance to both work and family. For him, these are the two wheels that drive the vehicle of life forward.

## The Challenge of Balance in Today's World

In today's fast-paced world, most people complain about the lack of time. Office work has increased to such an extent that they cannot spend quality time with their families. This often leads to stress, weakening relationships. However, Chacha Chaudhary's story teaches us that the solution to this stress lies in **balance.**

## Chacha Chaudhary's Approach to Balance

Chacha Chaudhary's life is never limited to just work or just family. He knows that focusing only on work will take away the happiness at home, and staying only at home will leave responsibilities unfulfilled. That's why he follows a unique **time management strategy** that helps him fulfil both equally well.

According to Chacha Chaudhary, every morning, we should prioritize the most important tasks of the day. This ensures we don't waste time on unnecessary activities and can spend meaningful moments with our families. For him, no matter how important work is, **spending time with family is the most crucial part of life.**

He has always followed the principle that when he is with his family, he is **completely present**—free from work-related stress or distractions.

## Maintaining Mental and Physical Balance

Another important rule for a happy family is maintaining a balance between mental and physical health. Chacha Chaudhary believes in cherishing small moments of joy and enjoying them to the fullest. For him, laughter, health, and happiness are as important as work.

This philosophy is what keeps his family organized, happy, and truly deserving of the title **Super Family**. And it's a lesson we can all learn to create harmony in our own lives!

### A Super Family is Built on Small Joys and Balance

To create a super family, we must learn to find happiness not just in big achievements but also in small moments. Chacha Chaudhary has always enjoyed laughter, games, and little activities with his family. According to him, these small things are the real essence of family happiness and success.

If we, too, can strike a balance between work and family, we can transform our lives into a joyful and fulfilling experience. Spending time with family, cherishing small joys, and managing time effectively are the keys to achieving both success and happiness in life.

### Lessons from Chacha Chaudhary's Super Family

Chacha Chaudhary's story teaches us that if you want your family to become a super family, you need to embrace his "Balance Mantra." It's not just about hard work; it's about working smart and maintaining love and connection with your family.

By doing so, you not only bring balance into your life but also pave the way for a happier, more fulfilling, and successful journey with your loved ones.

## 2.10 Chacha Chaudhary and Sabu's 8+8+8 Formula: The Secret to a Healthy, Wealthy, and Wise Life

One day, Chacha Chaudhary and Sabu were relaxing in their garden. Sabu had recently started paying attention to his daily routine and realized that he wasn't able to maintain balance. Sometimes he would overwork, and other times he would relax so much that important tasks would be left undone.

**Sabu** (curiously): "Chacha Ji, I've noticed that you always manage to stay balanced. You complete your work on time, get proper rest, and handle everything so well. How do you do it?"

**Chacha Chaudhary** (smiling): "Sabu, it's all thanks to living a balanced lifestyle. And for that, I follow a very simple formula called the '8+8+8 Formula.'"

And so, with Chacha Chaudhary's formula, Sabu found the way to make his life balanced, successful, and joyful.

**Sabu (in surprise):** "8+8+8? What's that, Chacha Ji?"

**Chacha Chaudhary** explained, "It's a simple formula where the 24 hours of a day are divided into three parts: 8 hours for sleep, 8 hours for work or studies, and 8 hours for rest, entertainment, and self-care. If you apply this formula in your life, not only will your life become balanced, but you will also become healthy, wealthy, and wise."

**Sabu:** "Hmm... So, this means I need to dedicate equal time to these three things every day?"

**Chacha Chaudhary** (nodding): "Absolutely right! But it's not just about dividing time; it's also about managing it properly. Let me explain it to you in detail."

### The First 8 Hours: Sleep – The Foundation of a Healthy Life

**Chacha Chaudhary:** "Let's first talk about sleep. Our body and mind need at least 8 hours of sleep to function properly. When you sleep, your body repairs itself, your brain processes the day's information, and your immune system gets stronger. If you don't complete your sleep, it affects your health, mood, and work. That's why 8 hours of sleep is essential."

**Sabu:** "Yes, Chacha Ji, I've noticed that when I don't get enough sleep, I feel tired all day and can't focus on my work."

**Chacha Chaudhary (seriously):** "That's absolutely correct. Lack of sleep doesn't just cause fatigue; in the long term, it can lead to serious health issues like heart problems, high blood pressure, and stress. So, there should never be any compromise on sleep."

**The Next 8 Hours: Work or Study – The Path to Wealth and Wisdom**

**Chacha Chaudhary:** "Now let's talk about the next 8 hours, which are for your work or studies. These 8 hours are crucial for your productivity. Whether you're studying or working, this time is very important. This is when you can enhance your skills, learn something new, and advance your career. I call it the 'Wealth and Wisdom' time."

**Sabu (excitedly):** "Got it! So, this is the time when I should focus completely on my work to achieve my goals. But Chacha Ji, if I have a lot of work, can I give more than 8 hours to it?"

**Chacha Chaudhary (smiling smartly):** "That's where the real balance lies, Sabu! If you spend more time working on some days, it will affect the rest of your schedule. Overworking will leave you with less time for sleep or self-care. That's why it's essential to manage your tasks smartly so that you don't need to work beyond these 8 hours. Overworking isn't good; it puts unnecessary stress on your body and mind."

## The Last 8 Hours: Self-Care and Entertainment – The Key to a Happy Life

**Chacha Chaudhary (calmly):** "Now let's talk about the last 8 hours, which are the most important for you – these are your 'rest and recovery' hours. During this time, you can do anything that brings you happiness and balance. For example, exercising, eating healthy food, spending time with your friends and family, or anything else that keeps you happy from within. This is the time for self-care."

**Sabu (smiling):** "Got it, Chacha Ji! So, this is the time to recharge myself and enjoy the things I love while maintaining balance in life."

**Sabu:** "So, this is the time when I can relax and focus on my hobbies, right?"

**Chacha Chaudhary (nodding in agreement):** "Exactly! These 8 hours are for your mental and physical well-being. If you don't set aside time for rest and entertainment in your daily routine, stress will slowly build up, and your life will become unbalanced. That's why these 8 hours deserve as much importance as work and sleep."

## Balance Is the True Key to Success

**Sabu:** "Chacha Ji, I completely understand now what this 8+8+8 rule means. If I give equal time to all three parts every day, my life will truly become balanced. I'll stay healthy, happy, and successful in my work."

**Chacha Chaudhary (proudly):** "Well done, Sabu! That's the right way. When you live a balanced life, every aspect of it naturally falls into place. Remember, health, wealth, and wisdom come only when you take care of yourself and use your time wisely."

**Sabu (laughing):** "Chacha Ji, now I will definitely follow this formula in my daily life."

**Chacha Chaudhary (smiling):** "Just follow this method, and see, success will follow you."

---

## Topic 2.11 - The Difference Between Understanding and Remembering: Logic vs Facts

One day, Chacha Chaudhary was sitting in his garden reading the newspaper when Chhotu came to him, looking upset from studying. Chhotu said, "Chacha Ji, I have a question that I can't understand. When I study, I always have to remember things. You might have a mind like Chacha Chaudhary's, but sometimes I don't understand what's logic and what's just something I have to memorize."

Chacha Chaudhary smiled and said, "Ah, Chhotu, that's the biggest difference between understanding (comprehension) and memorization. Let me tell you a story to explain."

### The Game of Logic and Facts

Chacha Chaudhary began explaining to Chhotu, who was sitting under a tree, "Suppose two questions come up in front of you. The first question is, 'Why does it rain?' and the second question is, 'What is the capital of India?' Now tell me, which of these questions is related to logic and which one to facts?"

Chhotu thought for a while and said, "Why rains is related to logic because we need to understand how clouds are formed and how water falls. And the capital of India is something we just have to remember."

Chacha Chaudhary nodded and said, "That's right! When the question starts with 'why' or 'how,' we need to understand the logic behind it. For example, the reason for rain is that the heat of the sun causes water to evaporate, which forms clouds, and then it rains. That's logic. But when the question starts with 'who,' 'what,' 'where,' or 'when,' the answer needs to be remembered as a fact."

## The Importance of Understanding and Memorization

Chhotu asked, "But Chacha ji, why do we need logic if we can just memorize everything?"

Chacha Chaudhary, with a slight smile, replied, "Look, son, it's important to remember facts because we need to know the information that has already been established to give the correct answers. But if you don't understand logic, sometimes answering questions when they are rephrased will become difficult. For example, if someone asks you 'What is the capital of India?' you can answer because it's a fact. But if they ask, 'Why is Delhi the capital of India?' you won't be able to answer by just memorizing the fact."

## The Combination of Logic and Facts

Sabu, who had been quietly listening, spoke up, "So, Chacha ji, we should remember both logic and facts?"

Chacha Chaudhary replied, "Absolutely right! In studies, it's essential to balance both logic and facts. If you understand a scientific principle, that's logic. But remembering dates or specific names related to that principle is a fact. When both come together, only then can you fully answer a question."

### Example: Why is there Snow on Mountains?

Chhotu asked, "Chacha ji, give me one more example."

Chacha Chaudhary said, "Suppose the question is, 'Why is there snow on mountains?' This is related to logic. The answer would be that at higher altitudes, the temperature is lower, causing the water droplets to freeze. But if the question is, 'What is the highest mountain in the world?' that's a fact-based question, and the answer is Mount Everest."

Chhotu, understanding the concept, said, "Now I understand the difference between logic and facts."

Chacha Chaudhary said, "As Aristotle said, 'The true purpose of knowledge is to understand, not just to memorize.' We should focus on understanding rather than just memorizing, because only then can we truly gain education."

Chacha Chaudhary concluded, "This is not just important for students, but also for parents to understand that children should focus on understanding things, not just memorizing them."

"When we understand something, it stays in our mind for a long time, and when we need it, we can recall it. This is why it is important to teach both logic and facts in a structured way."

---

## Topic 2.12 - Chacha Chaudhary and Sabu's Conversation: Education - Right or Privilege

When we hear the word "education," it immediately brings memories of books, school, and exams to our minds. As children, under the weight of books, we have all probably wondered at some point, is education really that important? But as we grow older, we realize that education is not just a formality, but the foundation on which our future stands. It not only helps us score good marks but also prepares us to distinguish between right and wrong, be aware of our rights, and become responsible citizens of society.

I still remember when I used to read Chacha Chaudhary's stories during my childhood. His sharp intellect and wise stories always inspired me. Reading his stories made me realize that in life, it's not just strength, but education and wisdom that can help accomplish great things. Each of Chacha Chaudhary's stories taught me something new, whether it was about scientific inventions or life's truths. This is the true meaning of education – it's not just about providing knowledge, but teaching us to approach every aspect of life with wisdom and understanding.

However, even today, many people in our society view education as a privilege, something meant only for a select few. Should this really be the case? Is education the right of only the rich, or should it be the birthright of every child? To answer this question, we need to think in a new direction.

One day, Chacha Chaudhary and Sabu were strolling through the streets of their village. Suddenly, they heard a child crying. When they approached, they saw a boy sitting with a bag of books in his hand, crying. Chacha Chaudhary asked him, "What happened, son? Why are you crying?"

The boy replied with a choked voice, "Chacha ji, I want to go to school, but my parents say that I should work to earn money. They believe education is not meant for us, and people like us should focus on earning a living instead of studying."

Hearing this, Chacha Chaudhary's heart melted. Smiling, he said to the boy, "Do you know, when I was of your age, I also used to feel the same way sometimes. But my parents explained to me that education is a right for everyone; it's not just a privilege. If we pursue education, we can create better opportunities for ourselves."

Sabu, in his deep voice, added, "Look, Chacha Chaudhary's mind is so sharp because he is educated. If he weren't educated, he wouldn't be able to solve every problem so easily."

The boy looked at Chacha Chaudhary in surprise and asked, "Chacha ji, is education really that important?"

Chacha Chaudhary nodded and said, "Absolutely. Education doesn't just provide knowledge from books; it teaches you how to think, understand, and solve your problems. It is your right, not a privilege. If you have education, you have all the power you need to succeed in life."

That day, the boy decided that he would study no matter what challenges came his way. He had understood that education is not just a privilege for the wealthy but a right for every child.

· Education cannot be a privilege only for those who can afford it. It is a right for every child and every individual. Education not only provides us with knowledge but also makes us better human beings and responsible citizens for a better society. Therefore, we must ensure that every child has the right to education so they can succeed in life and contribute to a brighter future for the country.

As the great thinker Nelson Mandela once said, ***"Education is the most powerful weapon you can use to change the world."*** With this thought in mind, we must ensure that education becomes a right for everyone, not just a privilege for a few.

## Topic 2.13 - The Role of Mnemonics in Life, Personality, and Career

Mnemonics play a very important role in life. They help improve and enhance our memory skills. Chacha Chaudhary's intellect is sharper than a computer because he uses his brain to its full potential. He has a special "mental trick" that helps him quickly solve even the most complex problems. Similarly, mnemonics act as a powerful tool for our memory.

### Chacha Ji's Mnemonic Tips for Life:

#### Making the Impossible Seem Possible

When Chacha Chaudhary faces a complex situation, he uses his sharp mind to find a simple solution. Mnemonics work the same way. They help us break down large and difficult facts into smaller, more manageable parts to remember easily. For example, to memorize a verse or facts, we can use certain keywords or abbreviations.

### Enhancing Memory (Sabu's Powerful Support)

Chacha Chaudhary has Sabu, who enhances his strength. Similarly, mnemonics amplify the power of our brain. When we organize information using mnemonics, our memory becomes sharper, making it easier to retain things. For instance, using "VIBGYOR" to remember the colours of the rainbow—each letter represents a colour.

### Remembering Long Lists (Chacha Chaudhary's Diary)

Chacha Chaudhary always carries a diary where he notes down important information. Mnemonics act like a mental diary for us. They help us memorize long lists effortlessly. For example, remembering the Great Lakes using **"HOMES"** (Huron, Ontario, Michigan, Erie, Superior).

### Associating with Familiar Things (Chacha Chaudhary's Local Knowledge)

Chacha Chaudhary connects new concepts to his familiar experiences for better understanding. Mnemonics work the same way. By linking new information to what we already know, we can recall it more easily. For example, when learning new words in a foreign language, we can connect them with words we are already familiar with.

### Conclusion

Just as Chacha Chaudhary's sharp intellect and Sabu's strength solve every problem, mnemonics are a magical tool for retaining memory and knowledge in our lives. They enable our brain to remember even the most complex information with ease, helping us become smarter and more successful in life.

### Chacha Ji's Mnemonic Tips for Career:

**Sabu:** "Chacha Ji, what role do mnemonics play in a career? Are they only useful for studies?"

**Chacha Chaudhary:** "Oh, Sabu, mnemonics are not just for studies; they are equally valuable in careers. Nowadays, every field demands more information and faster work. In such cases, mnemonics can become your superpower."

**Sabu:** "How, Chacha Ji? Does memory play such a significant role in every profession?"

**Chacha Chaudhary:** "Absolutely, Sabu. Memory is crucial in every profession. Let me give you a few examples to show how mnemonics have a big role in careers."

---

## In the Corporate World:

"Sabu, in large corporations, people attend numerous meetings, prepare reports, and interact with clients daily. Remembering every small detail can be challenging. By using mnemonics, they can quickly and effectively retain complex information for a long time. This improves their efficiency and effectiveness at work."

---

## In the Education Sector:

"Teachers and professors can use mnemonics to simplify complex topics for students. This not only increases students' interest in learning but also enhances their performance. Teachers who employ mnemonics often become more inspiring and impactful for their students."

---

## In the Medical Field:

"Doctors and medical students need to remember a vast amount of information—medicine names, disease symptoms, and much more. With the help of mnemonics, they can quickly memorize essential details and reduce the chances of errors."

## Conclusion:

From corporate offices to classrooms and hospitals, mnemonics can transform how professionals remember and process information. Just as Chacha Chaudhary's intelligence and Sabu's strength solve every problem, mnemonics can be the ultimate tool for career success, making work faster, more accurate, and impactful.

---

## In Law and Advocacy:

"Lawyers need to memorize case laws, constitutional sections, and complex arguments. Mnemonics can help them retain this vast information effortlessly and present everything fluently in court without relying heavily on notes."

---

**In Public Speaking and Leadership: "Sabu, when leaders deliver speeches, they have limited time and must remember their points in an impactful manner. Here, mnemonics prove invaluable, allowing them to present their speeches more effectively and win the hearts of their audience."**

---

## In Sales and Marketing:

"Salespeople and marketing professionals must understand their products thoroughly and cater to customers' needs efficiently. By using mnemonics, they can quickly recall and explain the features of their products to clients in a clear and concise manner."

---

## Conclusion:

**Sabu:** "Chacha Ji, this is truly amazing! Mnemonics play such a significant role in every profession?"

**Chacha Chaudhary:** "Absolutely, Sabu. Mnemonics simplify your tasks, and when work becomes easier, you progress faster in your career. Enhancing memory is a powerful tool for any professional."

**Sabu:** "Chacha Ji, you're absolutely right. I'm thinking of adopting mnemonics in my work. It will surely make tasks faster and more accurate!"

**Chacha Chaudhary:** "Indeed, Sabu. If you want to excel in your career quickly, mnemonics is a tool you must adopt. Learn the art of using it correctly, and you'll see how you shine in your field!"

Sabu asks Chacha Ji, "Chacha Ji, I've heard that mnemonics not only help in studies and work but also improve one's personality. Is that true?"

Chacha Chaudhary replies, "Absolutely true, Sabu! Mnemonics is not just a technique for remembering things; it can also enhance your overall personality. Let me explain how."

Sabu says, "Chacha Ji, this sounds a bit strange to me. What's the connection between memory and personality?"

Chacha Chaudhary explains, "Look, Sabu, personality is not just about outward appearances. It includes your thinking, confidence, and communication skills as well. Mnemonics can improve all of these aspects. Let me tell you about its benefits."

One of the most important benefits is **boosting confidence**. Chacha Ji says, "When you use mnemonics to remember things quickly and accurately, your confidence naturally increases. For example, if you're in a meeting or an interview and can speak fluently without referring to notes, people appreciate you. Confidence is the most essential part of a strong personality."

### The Art of Working Smartly:

"With mnemonics, you can remember complex information in an easy and fun way. This makes people think that you are smarter and quicker. For example, I use my 'Calendar Method' to quickly recall any date, and people think my memory is faster than a computer!"

### Better Communication Skills:

"Sabu, when you can easily remember things, you become more effective in conversations. When you can share the right examples, facts, or stories without hesitation, people are drawn to you and listen attentively. This positively impacts your communication skills and personality."

### Organization and Discipline:

"One special benefit of learning mnemonics is that it teaches your brain organization and discipline. When you remember everything in a pattern or system, your ability to think becomes more organized. And a person with organized thinking always has an impressive personality."

Here's the content translated into easy and readable English:

---

### Reducing Stress:

"People often feel stressed because of memory weaknesses. But if you use mnemonics, you'll experience less stress. For example, when I find myself in a difficult situation, I quickly solve the problem by using my memory and mnemonics. The ability to work without stress further enhances your personality."

### A Strong Public Image:

"When I speak without any paper, people think I am even smarter. Mnemonics also greatly impact your public image.

When people see how efficiently you remember and share information, they are drawn to you more."

**Sabu:** "Wow, Chacha Ji! So, mnemonics are not just a way to improve memory, but they also help enhance one's personality!"

**Chacha Chaudhary:** "Exactly, Sabu! If you want to improve your personality, start using mnemonics. Not only will your memory become sharper, but you'll also develop more confidence, organization, and an attractive personality."

**Sabu:** "So, I should also include mnemonics in my daily routine so that my personality can improve too!"

**Chacha Chaudhary:** "You're absolutely right, Sabu! Memory and personality are both connected. The sharper your mind is, the more impressive your personality will be."

---

## Topic 2.14 - Easy Ways for Smart Studying: Chacha Chaudhary's Lesson

One day, Chacha Chaudhary was sitting in his courtyard, surrounded by many children. All the children were discussing their studies. At that moment, Sabu eagerly said, "Chacha Ji, the children want to know how to easily remember difficult words and big answers."

Chacha Chaudhary smiled and looked at all the children carefully, then said, "You all are very smart, and making study methods easier is absolutely possible for you. Let me tell you a few special methods, by following which you can easily remember even the toughest things."

### 1. Simplification:

Chacha Chaudhary began to explain, "The first method is simplification, which means recognizing the main words in an answer or story and breaking it down into smaller points. For example, Mahatma Gandhi started the Satyagraha movement. Here, the key words are 'Mahatma Gandhi' and 'Satyagraha'. The rest of the words are just filler words, which you can create on your own."

Sabu said, "Wow, Chacha Ji, this will be so easy for the kids!"

Chacha Chaudhary continued, "Once we identify the keywords, we no longer have to worry about the other words. It becomes much easier to remember.

## 2. Tabulation:

"The next step is tabulation," Chacha Ji explained, "This method is useful when we need to organize several keywords in a table format. For example, if you want to remember countries' name and their capitals, you can create a table with the countries on one side and their capitals on the other. Like this: India - Delhi, Japan - Tokyo."

The children clapped and said, "This is a fun method!"

## 3. Conversion:

Chacha Ji took out some paper and gave an example, "Now, if you're struggling to remember a word that doesn't have a clear image in your mind, you can turn it into an image using your imagination. For example, to remember Galileo, we can imagine 'Leo in the alley,' where Leo means a lion wandering in the alley. This way, you'll easily remember Galileo."

Sabu laughed and said, "Wow! This is fun, Chacha Ji!"

## 4. Association:

Finally, Chacha Ji explained, "Now the most important step is Association, which means linking keywords with stories or images. For example, when you hear the name Agra, the image of the beautiful Taj Mahal immediately comes to your mind.

Similarly, if we connect words through stories, they will never be forgotten."

Chacha Chaudhary gave another example, "For instance, if we need to remember 'bauxite' and 'Australia,' we can imagine a kangaroo boxing. This will make both words stick in our minds forever."

After hearing all of this, the children clapped and said happily, "Chacha Ji, now we can easily remember big answers and difficult words!"

Chacha Chaudhary smiled and said, "Remember, studies should always be done in a smart way. As the famous philosopher Confucius once said, 'I hear and I forget, I see and I remember, I do and I understand.' So, always make the learning process easy and full of fun."

All the children, excited, said, "Now we will study with Chacha Chaudhary's techniques, and we will never forget anything!"

## Topic 2.15 - Bini Chachi Made Tea and Boosted Everyone's Memory at Home

Chacha Ji was sitting with the children, and they were asking him ways to make studying fun and easy. Billu asked, "Chacha Ji, is it possible to remember things without rote learning and without repeating them over and over again? Or is there a way that we can remember things without trying, and they just come to us naturally?"

Chacha Ji replied, "Yes, absolutely! Your mind has a power, and there is a technique called 'Association.' If you link your studies or whatever you want to remember with your daily activities or routine in your imagination, it will be much easier to recall, and this will become a fun activity as well."

Billu then asked, "How? Can you give an example?"

Chacha Ji said, "Alright, what subject do you find difficult to remember? History?"

Billu quickly replied, "Yes!"

**Chacha Ji said, "Let's make history fun and memorable without rote learning today." As Chacha Ji opened Billu's history book, he said, "Here is a topic: Important Information about the Harappa Civilization. Now, how do you all usually remember this?"**

TEA MAKING METHOD

All the children said together, "We all cram, Chacha Ji!"

"Yes, yes, yes," replied Chacha Ji, and all the children laughed together. Chacha Ji then said, "If you connect this topic to some routine in your life, it won't feel like cramming anymore; instead, you'll remember it automatically."

The children asked, "How?"

Chacha Ji started thinking, and just then, Bini Chachi came in and said, "Listen, should I make some tea? Will you have tea?"

Chacha Ji snapped his fingers and said, "Oh yes, please make tea, and also boost the memory of all these children with your tea."

"How can tea boost memory? You and your strange ideas!" Bini Chachi said jokingly.

"Oh dear, this is the power of imagination in brain science," replied Chacha Ji. The children said, "Chacha Ji, tell us how tea will improve our memory and how we'll remember this topic." Chacha Chaudhary replied, "Alright, let's all watch Bini Chachi making tea, and I'll explain how making tea can become a method—The Tea-Making Method.

We'll connect the tea-making process with an imaginary story and link it to your study topic, the Harappa Civilization. You'll see how amazing this method is. It will be easy, and it's a method you can easily create on your own. You can use your normal routine activities, things you see around you, and things you do, and by doing so, you can make methods to remember your study content.

Today, I will teach you about the Harappa Civilization. First, let's look at it in a normal way, just like a teacher explains it. We will identify the key points and separate the main keywords."

- **Harappa spread in the Indus Valley Civilization.**
- **It was discovered in 1921.**
- **It was discovered by Professor Dayaram Sahni.**
- **It developed in Pakistan.**
- **It spread near the Ravi River.**
- **Wheat was also found in this civilization.**
- **Cotton was also found in this civilization.**
- **Punching stamps were also used for trading in this civilization.**
- **A picture of an ox was also found, meaning farming was done using oxen.**
- **Shells were also found.**
- **Copper was also found in the Harappa Civilization.**

History teachers teach us like this and explain it to us. Here, we get confused about which civilization had what findings. Remembering all the points becomes a little difficult, and if we write all the points of any civilization together, we end up repeating or memorizing them multiple times.

But today, I will share a technique of the mind that will help you understand and remember it forever. Our method is called the **Tea-Making Method**. Now, you'll tell your parents, "From today, I'll make tea!"

Making tea has a specific process. Have you ever heard of someone first adding tea leaves, boiling them, and then adding water afterward? No, because making tea follows a proper sequence.

First, what do you do to make tea? You go to the kitchen. Then, you take a tea pot where tea is prepared. Next, you pour water into it and place it on the stove. You look for a lighter to turn on the stove and let the water heat slightly. After that, you add tea leaves and sugar, let it boil for a while, and then add milk. You let it simmer for some time, and once the tea is ready, you strain it into a cup.

Tell me, kids, do you know this is exactly how tea is made, right? Your mom follows the same process when she makes tea at home, doesn't she? We strain the tea into a cup or a jug and then enjoy it with full delight!

Now, let's connect tea-making to remembering the Harappa Civilization. Imagine, kids, if your exam is tomorrow, instead of rote memorizing like others, you'll simply revise using this tea-making method.

Imagine this: A Sardarji comes to your house and says, 'Oye Harappa, I will only drink tea made by you! I want tea, and I won't leave without it!'"

First, you go to the kitchen to make tea, and you think to yourself that you want to serve tea to Sardarji uncle in a special way. You seat him on the sofa and say, 'Wait, let me bring the tea.' But then he says, 'Oye Harappa, hurry up and bring the tea!'

When you go to the kitchen, you notice that a net is placed over the gas with a lot of oranges on it. Because of the net, you can't even see the gas. You lift the net and move the oranges aside. Now, when you try to make tea, you realize that you can't find the tea pot. You get really worried because if you don't find the pot, you won't be able to make the tea, and Sardarji uncle will get upset.

So, you remember Lord Ram and pray, 'Oh Lord Ram, please help me find the pot quickly.' As you prayed, Lord Ram shows his grace, and the tea pot appears in your hand. You thank Lord Ram, saying, 'Thank you, Lord Ram, for your mercy and kindness!'

Then you placed the pot on the gas and started adding water. As soon as you added the water, a small spark (like small flag) emerged from it. Where was it from? It was from Pakistan! You thought, 'Wow, this is some magical water from which a spark with stars and moons came out.' You picked it up and placed it aside.

Next, when you tried to light the gas, you couldn't find the lighter. You searched for it, and then you saw your friend Ravi standing by a river with a lighter, smoking a cigarette. Smoking is a harmful habit. 'Smoking is injurious to health!' you thought, and immediately ran over to him. You snatched the cigarette from his hand and threw it into the river. Then, you took the lighter and scolded him, saying, 'You should never smoke! It's a bad habit!'

You took the lighter and used it to light the gas. As soon as the gas was lit, wheat started coming out of the burner, so much wheat that your entire kitchen was filled!

Then, you allowed the water to heat up, and after that, you were supposed to add tea leaves. When you looked for the tea leaves box and opened it, you found that it was filled with cotton! Can you believe it? Cotton in the tea leaves box! You removed the cotton, and finally, the tea leaves were there.

After that, you opened the sugar box to add sugar, but inside, someone had placed punching stamps. You removed the stamps and added the sugar. You let the tea boil, and as the tea started to boil, a big bull appeared from the boiling tea! The bull said, "I'll also drink tea." You said, "Alright, fine, sit with Chacha ji and enjoy your tea."

You let the tea boil for a while, and then you needed to add milk. You opened the fridge to get the milk, but there was no milk in the pots. However, you found milk in the conch, so you took the milk from there and added it to the tea.

Then the tea started cooking and a wonderful fragrance began to spread. Suddenly, you heard a voice from inside, "Harappa, the tea smells really good, hurry up and bring it!" You strained the tea, and for uncle, you poured it into a copper mug, and for the bull, you poured it into a large copper jug. The container you used for straining the tea was also made of copper.

Then, you went to the drawing room and served the tea to uncle and the bull. They both tasted it and said, "Wow, the tea is really good!"

Now, let's see what's relevant in this story.

Bini Chachi said, "Kids, I'm sure you understood now because your mind works like Chacha Chaudhary's mind, with the new technique!"

Chacha Chaudhary laughed and said, "Let's understand it better and see what we remember."

First, who came to your house to drink tea? Akal, who said, "I'll drink Harappa's tea." So, from Harappa, what did we remember? The main word is **Harappa Civilization**.

Next, we encountered **oranges** and **nets**. As I mentioned before, using the Vibgyor Method, the colour of the **orange** is 19, and the phonetic method gives **net** the number 21. (In other chapters of this book, you can learn the Vibgyor and phonetic methods and understand this technique well.)

**19 - Orange (Vibgyor Method)**
**21 - NET (Phonetic Method)**
**1921 - Orange and Net**

The discovery of the Harappa Civilization happened in 1921.

After that, you couldn't find the **bhagona** (vessel), so you asked **Lord Ram** for help. This reminds us that, just like Chacha Chaudhary's brain, the discovery could have been yours too. **Professor Dayaram Sahni** asked for **Lord Ram's** blessings. So, this will remind you of **Dayaram Sahni**.

After you added water and a twig from Pakistan came out, it will remind you that this developed in Pakistan. Then, when you couldn't find the lighter that Ravi had taken to the riverbank, it will remind you of the **Ravi River**, which spread along the riverbank.

When you lit the gas and first found a lot of **wheat**, this is evidence that wheat was found. It shows that people of the **Harappan Civilization** grew wheat, and this is proof.

Now, tell me children, when you were making tea, the next step was to add the tea leaves. When you opened the tea box and found **cotton**, it tells us that the people of the Harappan Civilization grew **cotton**. They wore clothes made from **cotton**.

After that, when you added sugar and opened the sugar box, you found **bird footprints**. This shows that they used **bird stamps** for trading in the **Harappan Civilization**.

Next, when the tea boiled and a **bull** appeared, it reminds us of the **bull picture** found in the **Harappan Civilization**. This shows they used bulls for farming.

Now, what happened next, children? Tell me quickly!

The tea was boiling and turning black, so what did we need to add next? Milk. Where did we add the milk? In a **shell**. We added the milk from the shell. This is important to remember because what usually happens in tea-making is becoming strange and unusual, and the strange thing is the answer to our question.

This is the magic of this method. Now, what will you remember from this? When we added milk from the shell, it indicates that people of the **Harappan Civilization** used to worship God with the **shell**. Shells were found in the Harappan Civilization.

Next, when you strained the tea into a copper mug, it will remind you that **copper metal** was also found in the Harappan Civilization.

Now, children, when you think about making tea, you will remember the answer. When you add the milk, you will remember the **shell**. When you open the tea box, you will remember **cotton**. So, by thinking of the entire process of making tea, you will remember all the answers to this question.

Whenever you need to revise, you don't need to memorize. Just think about making tea with **Bini Chachi** or make it yourself!

This is also a way to remember any question. First, read it as it is, so that the key words will stick in your mind. The second step is to remember the answer using a technique, such as memory techniques, where we turn everything into a picture or image format.

But children, when you need to revise it, first use the same technique you used to convert it into a picture format and revise it that way. Then, read the key words. I guarantee, children, that this answer will never leave your mind.

For other children, there is a historical topic that is boring, and for you, this is an activity.

Now, you may think that since we've remembered Harappa, let's try something else. Similarly, you can use this technique to remember anything while making or doing something. For example, if you're wondering how to remember Kali Banga, start by thinking about how you make Maggi—starting from the beginning to the end. Apply the same technique and remember it. In this way, you can link any question or answer with any technique, whether it's about making food or anything else.

Children, everything has a process, and by following that process, we can remember not just one thing but many things. We can use the same method to boost our memory. Isn't it fun, this technique?

Chacha Chaudhary said, and all the children said together, "Wow, Chacha Ji, that was fun! It's remembered! Your mind works the same way as your technique. Wow!"

## Topic 2.16 - Chacha Chaudhary's Rainbow Trick to Remember History

Chacha Ji asked the children, "Hey kids, why are you so happy?"

The children jumped in excitement, "Chacha Ji, look at that! Look at the sky, it's such a beautiful sight, so many wonderful colours blooming in the sky!"

Chacha Ji looked up at the sky and said, "Wow, that does look very beautiful."

Being a great intellectual, he asked the children, "Children, do you know the names of the colours of the rainbow? Do you know the sequence of these rainbow colours?"

The children laughed and said, "Oh Chacha Ji, that's such an easy question! We already know how to remember the rainbow colours and their sequence. We know both!"

Chacha Ji asked, "Oh really? So, tell me, how will you remember them?"

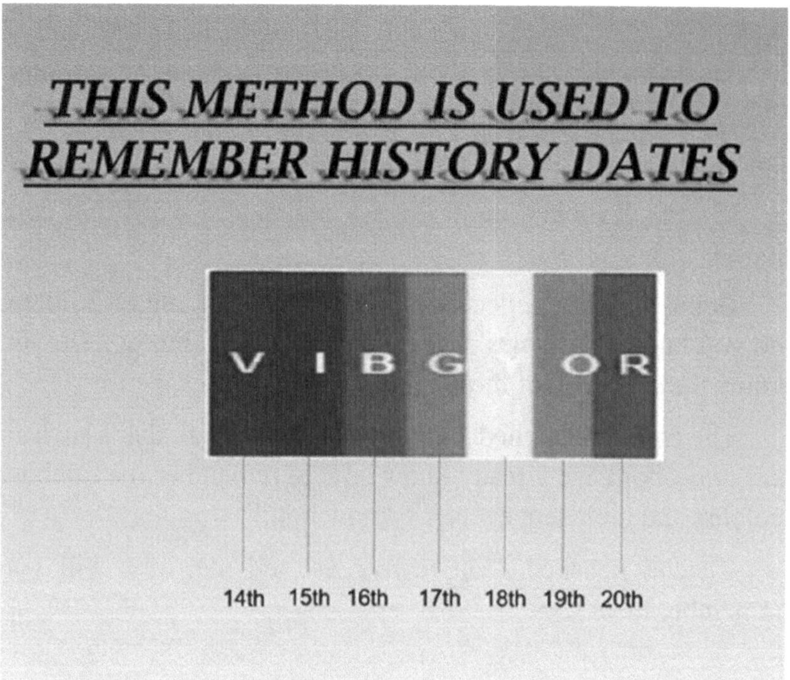
THIS METHOD IS USED TO
REMEMBER HISTORY DATES
V I B G
O R
14th 15th 16th 17th 18th 19th 20th

RAINBOW METHOD

The children were happy and said, "Mom told us that instead of remembering all the colour names, we can just remember one word, and that word is VIBGYOR."

V - Violet (Purple)

I - Indigo

B - Blue

G - Green

Y - Yellow

O - Orange

R - Red

"See, Chacha Ji, now we can easily remember the names and sequence of the rainbow colours!"

Chacha Ji was happy and said, "Wow, kids, you are really intelligent! Now tell me, have you ever remembered something else using the word 'VIBGYOR'?"

The children were surprised and said, "Something else? What else, Chacha Ji? We thought 'VIBGYOR' could only be used to remember the sequence and colours of the rainbow."

Chacha Ji replied, "No, dear, intelligent people use one tool for multiple purposes! Let me tell you how else you can use the word 'VIBGYOR'."

- First, you can use each letter of the word to remember the sequence of any long answer or paragraph.
- You can also use 'VIBGYOR' to remember historical dates and the centuries they belong to.

The children asked, "How, Chacha Ji? Please explain it clearly."

Chacha Ji said, "Alright, sit comfortably, and I will explain everything to you."

Chacha Chaudhary explained to the children, "Look children, remembering history dates can sometimes be a bit difficult because it involves several details, like the date, month, year, and century. When we remember history dates, there are mainly four things involved:

1. The date: The day of the month, from 1 to 31.
2. The month: Which month it is.
3. The year: The specific year.
4. The century: Which century it belongs to.

Any date is made from these four things. For example, let's understand this with an example...

**In 1857, the battle of Jhansi was fought**. It has 1800 as the century and 57 as the year.

Another example is...

**13th April, Jallianwala Bagh massacre**, which involves two things: the date and the month. In some cases, all four things are involved, like 15th August 1947, our Independence Day! This has all four: the day, month, year, and century. These four things can be remembered in different ways.

Now, if we need to remember the **century**, we can use the word **VIBGYOR.**

The children excitedly asked, "How, Chacha Ji? Please explain a bit more."

So, for now, I have found a method to remember the centuries from the 14th to the 20th, and that method is the **VIBGYOR Method**. Now, let's understand how we can do this.

You can connect the letters of the **VIBGYOR** word with the centuries!

For example:

- The colour code for the 14th century will be **Violet** (V).

- The colour code for the 15th century will be **Indigo** (I).
- The colour code for the 16th century will be **Blue** (B).
- The colour code for the 17th century will be **Green** (G).
- The colour code for the 18th century will be **Yellow** (Y).
- The colour code for the 19th century will be **Orange** (O).
- The colour code for the 20th century will be **Red** (R).

See, kids, it became easy to remember the century codes! Now, you can visualize each century in colours, which will make it easier to remember.

There are also other ways to remember different things, and I will teach you those on another day. Today, we made the **Rainbow Method** based on what we saw in the rainbow. We can create more methods for other things as we go. In this way, kids, we can connect everything that we can see with things that we can't see, and that will help us remember even things that are invisible to us.

Isn't it a fun way to remember things?

So, kids, remember, if you can see it, you'll remember it!

Now, let's play some more games, learn new things, and try to visualize and remember new information.

For example, **Gandhi Ji's birthday on 2nd October** is easy to remember, but kids sometimes get confused about his birth year. Gandhi Ji's birth year is **1869**.

I will now show you how to use the power of the mind and imagination to remember this.

Chacha Ji smiled and said, "Yes, kids, let me explain more! If you open your books, you will see that most of the history dates that need to be remembered are between the 14th century and the 20th century!"

In this, the century number is 18, and the year number is 69.

Using the **VIBGYOR Method**, 18 corresponds to **Yellow** (Y), and 69 can be remembered with the phonetic code **J and P**, which sounds like **Jeep**. So, when you say it together, it becomes **Yellow Jeep** (a yellow jeep).

(You can learn more about the phonetic method in the other chapters of this book and understand this method better.)

Imagine Gandhi Ji celebrating his birthday and traveling in a yellow jeep. The song "Happy Birthday" is playing, and the jeep is decorated for the celebration. Whenever you need to remember Gandhi Ji's birth year, you will think of the yellow jeep, and that will remind you of **1869**, solving the confusion.

Isn't this a great technique? Isn't it fun?

The kids are happy and running, thanking Chacha Ji.

## Topic 2.17 - Answers are hidden in Chacha Chaudhary's questions -

### Chacha Chaudhary's magical mind and the magic of memory

One day Chacha Chaudhary was sitting on the comfortable sofa in his house and was reading the newspaper, then his wife, Bini Chachi, asked him, "Chacha Ji, how do children remember so many things these days? Earlier we also used to go to school, but it was very difficult to remember so many things."

Chacha Chaudhary smiled and said, "Bini, think of children's minds as a house, just like in our house there is a separate place for everything - utensils in the kitchen, clothes in the cupboard, dining room for eating, bedroom for sleeping and store room for unnecessary things. Similarly, in the mind also every information has a place. The information which is kept in the right place, it never gets lost, but if the information is filled in the mind without any order and logic, it gets scattered and we think that we have forgotten. Actually, we do not forget anything, it is just that the information gets lost." It is just like it is still in memory but not able to remember.

Meanwhile, his friend Sabu also arrived there. He said to Chacha ji, "Chacha ji, I do not understand how do you remember so many things? Is there some magic in your mind?"

Chacha Chaudhary laughed and said, "Sabu, it's not magic, but the right learning technique.

"We should use our mind in the right way. Like now I will teach you a method, which is called **'Prashna Akshar Vidhi', (Question Letter Method)** with this method, we will never make a mistake in remembering the order of any question."

Sabu said in surprise, **"Prashna Akshar Vidhi? (Question Letter Method)** What is this?"

Chacha Chaudhary kept the newspaper aside and said, the human mind is like a house, and he starts explaining like there are rooms in a house. And different things are kept in different rooms. Everything is kept at a particular place which we keep after classifying it in a particular way, like utensils in the kitchen, clothes in the cupboard, sleeping beds in the bedroom, dining table in the dining room, there is a drawing room for guests, and a store room for unnecessary things etc.

The brain also works in the same way, the brain is the house of information, and the brain also uses logic in the same way to keep information. The information which is kept at its appropriate place according to logic is never lost, but the information which is kept at any place in the house of the brain without using logic, often gets misplaced in the brain and is not remembered, and we consider it as forgetting. In reality we do not forget anything, we just misplace the information.

We often make mistakes in remembering the order of answers memorized in a sequential manner. The information is present in the mind but we still get confused, even after remembering it many times, answers related to chronology always confuse us.

Let us also learn a method to remember such questions, it is called **Prashna Akshar Vidhi (Question Letter Method)**, as the name suggests we can use the letters of the question to remember the answer. As I had mentioned above that if a logical place is made to keep things in the house of the mind, then they will be placed at the designated place. In this method we will use the letters of the root word of the question as a logical platform. For example, the chronological list of the main kings of the Gupta dynasty is as follows, the first king is Shri Gupta, then Chandragupta, Samudragupta, Chandragupta Vikramaditya, Kumaragupta and Skanda Gupta respectively. Now we have to remember it in chronological order i.e. in this order, and that too forever. For this, you should look at the letters of the original word of the question, the original word spelling is G U P T A (Gupta), we can give an imaginary meaning to its letters and connect the answer with it. For example, the first letter is G and G for girl as an imaginary meaning, U for umbrella, P for parrot, T for tiger, and A for apple.

Now let us remember the order of the Gupta dynasty, Gupta is common in this order, so there is no need to remember it. Just remember the main names of the kings. The first king is Shri Gupta, we can logically assume that he was an institutional king, so the honory Shri is added to his name, so the name is Shri Gupta. After this comes Chandragupta, imagine that a G-girl is sitting on the moon. The next king is Samudragupta, imagine that in the middle of the sea there is a big U for umbrella. After this is Vikramaditya, imagine that instead of Betal, P for parrot is sitting on the back of King Vikram. The next king was Kumar Gupta, see there is a potter (Kumar) who is making big toys of clay, T for tiger. Last is Skanda Gupta, Skanda has two skandhs, (shoulders) and the letter A for apple, imagine that you have apples on both your shoulders. Now just think, to know who were the kings of the Gupta dynasty in order, you just have to focus on the letters of the question, like the first king we remembered from logic was 'Shri' Gupta. Because he is the first king, then who was there, just think of 'Girl', where was she sitting, on the moon, and you remembered Chandra Gupta, after that? U for umbrella, and you will remember Samudra Gupta. Isn't this logic amazing?

Sabu said excitedly, "Wow! This is a very easy and interesting method! Now I will never forget the kings of the Gupta dynasty."

Chacha Chaudhary said smilingly, "This method can be used with every question. When we connect the letters of a question with our imagination and logic, our mind always remembers that information."

Bini Chachi happily said, "You are really amazing! We all get to learn a lot from you."

Chacha Chaudhary finally said, "Remember, the real art is to use the brain in the right way. When we connect things in the right order and logic, then there is no problem of forgetting any information. Just organize your brain like a house and keep every information in its right place." And thus, Chacha Chaudhary proved once again that his brain works faster than a computer, and taught the children a new technique, so that they too never forget the correct answer to every question.

## Topic 2.18 - Chacha Chaudhary's Self Imagination Techniques, Makes You Remember in No time

When it comes to General Knowledge, everyone wants to remember it, but often it is so factual that it seems difficult to remember it. Chacha Chaudhary, whose brain is faster than a computer, solves such difficult questions very easily. One day, when all the children were worried about how to remember these General Knowledge facts, Chacha Chaudhary taught them in his unique way how General Knowledge can be easily remembered by using imagination and association.

Chacha Chaudhary once reached among the children with Sabu, where all the children were getting ready for the General Knowledge test. But the problem was that the children were not able to remember which thing is connected to what. Then Chacha Chaudhary smiled and said, "Why don't we remember it in the form of a game?"

First of all, Chacha Chaudhary talked about Jalandhar and sports equipment. He asked the children, "Imagine that all your sports equipment is floating inside water (JAL KE ANDAR). Now tell me, where is the sports equipment attached to?" The children immediately said, "Jalandhar!"

Then Chacha ji started the game of Katni and cement. He said, "Imagine that you have a cut (KAT) on your knee (NI) and you are applying cement on it instead of medicine. Now tell me, where does the cement come from?" The children laughed and said, "Katni!"

After this, Chacha Chaudhary gave the example of bushes (Jharia) and coal. He said, "Imagine that bushes (Jharia) are full of coal. Now tell me, where does the coal come from?" The children immediately said, "Jharia!"

Then, Chacha ji added Kerala and coffee. He said, "Imagine you are eating karela (bitter gourd) dipped in coffee. Now tell me, where does coffee come from?" All the children answered in unison, "Kerala!"

Next, it was the turn of Karnataka and rubber. Chacha Chaudhary said, "Your friend is giving you rubber toys and asking you to perform a play (NATAK KARO) on stage. Now tell me, where does rubber come from?" The children laughed and said, "Karnataka!"

Finally, Chacha Chaudhary connected West Bengal with rice and said, "Imagine a big bungalow (BANGLA) filled with lots of rice. Now tell me, where does the rice come from?" and the children immediately replied, "West Bengal!"

The children were very happy to be taught in this new and fun way. Chacha Chaudhary explained to them that when we connect facts with some imagination, it becomes difficult to forget them. With this method of association and imagination, everyone can easily remember the toughest facts of general knowledge.

And thus, Chacha Chaudhary proved once again that his brain really works faster than a computer!

## Topic 2.19 - Chacha Chaudhary has Google Map in his mind, he never forgets the way

Chacha Chaudhary's mind was no less than a computer, and this was the reason why he could solve difficult questions and problems very easily. One day, a group of children came to him and told him their problem. The problem was that whenever they went on a new path, they could not remember where to turn and where to go straight. They kept asking someone for directions again and again. Sabu also smiled after hearing this and Chacha Chaudhary said, "Oh this is very easy, come let me teach you a way by which you will never forget the way."

Chacha Chaudhary said to the children, "Your mind remembers information by associating it, and if we remember things by associating them with a picture or object, then we will never forget it. We call this the 'path visualization method."

Then Chacha Chaudhary started a story. He said, "Imagine you are driving your car in a new city and you have to go to your friend's house in Sarita Apartments, Sector 5. You ask someone for directions and they tell you: 'To go to Sector 5, go straight, then turn left at the red light, turn right after the hospital, right again at the post office, left at the big temple, take a U-turn in front of the school, turn left again after the police station. Turn right at the T-junction and then go straight across the intersection and take a U-turn under the flyover and you will reach Sector 5.

The children said, "This looks very complicated, Chacha ji!" Chacha Chaudhary laughed and said, "But don't worry, it is very easy to remember, just listen to me carefully." He explained to the children that there are only four main actions in every road – left turn, right turn, straight and U-turn. Now if we connect these actions with some easy imaginations, then we will never be forgetting the route.

For example: -

- Left turn = Leaf
- Right turn = Red
- U-turn = Umbrella
- Straight = As it is (no change)

Now let's use imagination to remember this entire route: -

1. Go straight - No need to add anything here.
2. Left from red light - Imagine that there are lots of leaves fallen on the red light.
3. Right after hospital - Imagine that the whole hospital is painted red.
4. Right from post office - Imagine that the post office has also turned red.

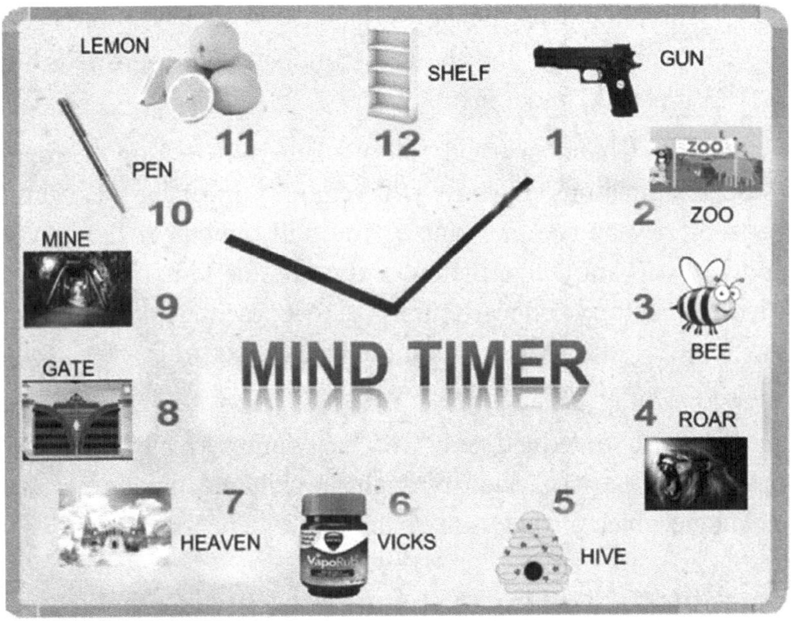
LEMON
SHELF
GUN
11
12
1
PEN
ZOO
10
2
ZOO
MINE
9
3
BEE
GATE
MIND TIMER
8
4
ROAR
7
6
5
HEAVEN
VapoRub
VICKS
HIVE

5. Left near the temple - Imagine that the temple is covered with leaves.
6. U-turn in front of the school - Imagine that there is a big umbrella over the school.
7. Left after the police station - There are leaves all around the police station.
8. Right at the T-junction - Here too the T-junction is painted red.
9. Cross the intersection straight - No need to remember anything here, just go straight.
10. U-turn under the flyover - Imagine that there is a big umbrella under the flyover.

Chacha Chaudhary said, 'Now when you walk on the road, these imaginations of yours will remind you of the next turn. As soon as you see the temple, you will remember the leaves and you will know that there is a river on the left. The children tried this method and were surprised that now they do not forget the route at all." All the children learnt this trick of Chacha Chaudhary and went on their way happily.

Sabu also smiled and said, "Chacha ji's brain is really amazing!" In this way, Chacha Chaudhary taught the children a unique memory technique which made forgetting the way a game for them.

## Topic 2.20 - Tips to sharpen the brain are hidden in every corner of Chacha Chaudhary's house

Let us understand the context of this topic through story of Chacha Chaudhary, one day Chacha ji was taking tea sitting in the drawing room. While taking tea, Chacha ji felt like eating biscuits. He asked his wife to bring a packet of biscuits.

She got worried and said, "Oh, the biscuits are finished, I went to the market but I still forgot, what should I do, whenever I go to buy things, I forget something or the other."

Chacha ji explained, "It is okay, it keeps happening, forgetting is human nature, it is not a big deal."

Still Chachi insisted and said, "These days I have started forgetting a lot, because of which I have a lot of trouble and it takes a lot of time."

Chacha ji said, "Forgetting is a human nature, which is natural, but it can be remembered in an unnatural way, that is, artificial way."

Chachi asked, "What did you say, artificial way, what do you mean? I did not understand what you are trying to say."

Chacha ji explained, "I will tell you a very beautiful thing related to the art of remembering, listen carefully. Whenever we want to remember something, it is not remembered." But the thing which gets memorized automatically, we remember that information only.

Chachi got a little confused and said- "I am not able to understand what are you saying. What is the relation of matter of forgetting biscuits with this, I did not understand."

Chacha ji said, "Today I am going to explain a very good thing to you, listen carefully, this thing is very useful for children also. We keep forgetting small things in our regular life. As you just told, there are 15 things in the shopping list, but when we go to the market, out of 15, only 5-7 are remembered and the rest we forget."

Chachi ji said with great satisfaction- "Yes, this keeps happening, it happens with everyone, there is no cure for it."

Chacha ji happily said- "No no, it is not like that.

"Today I will tell you a new way how you can remember your shopping list. You can do that too without forgetting a single item. Ok tell me one thing- Do you remember the room in which we are sitting?"

Chachi ji started laughing- "Hey, what are you joking about, what is there to remember about the room in which I am staying, I remember it, of course."

Chacha ji said, in technical language, "It is called live memory. If another memory is connected with a live memory, then we remember that too. This is called the principle of association, meaning two things getting connected with each other.

"Come, I will show you a practical.

"Suppose you have to go shopping today and there are items in your shopping list.

Banana

A dozen eggs

Newspaper

Teddy bear

Biscuit

Soap

Ball pen

Bucket

Staple

Mobile

"Now the biggest challenge is to remember all these lists, let's do it in an easy way.

"First of all, I will tell you what you can see in this room.

"First start from the door and start looking at it clockwise. See, first of all you can see the door."

Chachi replied, "Yes, I can see it. And, after the door, I can see this table."

Chacha ji moving forward, "After the table there is a window, after the window there is a showcase, after that there is a TV panel, a lamp is placed above the TV, if you look a little further you will see a washroom, if you go further, then you can see a dining table, after the dining table there is a crockery unit, after the crockery unit there is a kitchen gate, after the kitchen door can you see a big photo frame?"

Chachi ji smiling, "Yes, I can see it, look a little more above this photo frame and you will also see our ceiling fan."

Chacha ji, "Very good, it means you can see everything. Now tell me one thing, if you go to the market to buy goods and stand there and think about this room in the market itself, will you remember this thing?"

Chachi ji smiled and said, "Of course, I will be able to visualize, I watch this 50 times a day, this is my house, I remember it."

Chacha ji, smiled and said, "Come on, let me show you a magic. Just listen to what I say and visualize it."

1. **Door-** When you see the door, imagine that you are finding a big bundle of bananas hanging outside the door. (Attach the bananas to the door.)
2. **Table-** A carton of eggs is kept on the table and as soon as you try to touch it, all the eggs (a dozen eggs) fall here and there. (Attach the eggs to the table.)
3. **Window-** A paper is flying outside the window and this paper is actually your newspaper. (Attach the newspaper to the window.)
4. **Showcase-** A big teddy bear is kept inside the showcase, which is peeking from there. (Attach the teddy bear to the showcase.)
5. **TV panel-** A lot of Parle-G biscuits are kept on top of the TV panel, and as soon as you switch on the TV, they start falling. (Attach the Parle-G to the TV panel.)
6. **Lamp-** A strange kind of light is coming from the lamp and the smell of soap is felt from that light. (Attach the soap to the lamp.)
7. **Washroom-** A big ball pen is kept outside the washroom, as if someone has left it there by mistake. (Connect ball pen with washroom.)

8. **Dining table-** A bucket filled with water is placed on the dining table. (Connect bucket with dining table.)
9. **Crockery unit-** A stapler is placed inside the crockery unit, which is shining among the other utensils. (Connect stapler with the crockery unit.)
10. **Kitchen door-** A board is placed on the kitchen door, on which it is written that we have to go for mobile repair. (Connect mobile repair with kitchen door.)

"Now when you go to the market and visualize this room, all these things will come to your mind automatically.

"For example- When you think of door, you will remember banana. If you think of the table, you will remember eggs. As soon as you think of the window, you will think of the newspaper. You will see a teddy bear in the showcase. Parle-G biscuits on the TV panel. Soap on the lamp and other such items."

In this whole process, Chacha ji told a fun and practical way, by which you will be able to remember the whole list without any stress. This means that every time you think of any part of the room, you will also remember the shopping item associated with it.

Now all that has to be done is to practice this technique, so that whenever you have to remember something, you can easily remember it by associating things in this way.

## Topic 2.21 - Chacha Chaudhary's A B C D E Makes Brain Super Brain

Chacha Chaudhary always tells new methods to make children's studies easy and for their betterment with a new technique. He explains new methods and today we are understanding a new principle. He called all the children together and said, "Come on children, let's learn a new technique today which will help you to remember well to get good marks in studies." The children were very happy, and ssid, "Today we will learn a new thing from Chacha ji which will be very good for us in studies!!!"

"Children, everyone wants to get good marks in studies. And everyone is engaged in studies day and night to get good marks these days. There are four bases of studies to get good marks, reading, writing, understanding and remembering. The most important thing is to remember because it is your memory that is tested. Whatever you have read, written or understood, if you do not remember it in the exam, you will not get marks. And to remember it well and on time, it is important you should remember it well. The more firmly you memorize, the sooner you will remember it."

## The principle of A. B. C. D. E.

The information that the brain stores in visual form is stored as specific information and is remembered quickly. To make any information strong and specific, you should understand this principle and use it in your studies.

**A- Action**, the information which is in action form is better remembered by our brain.

Like we automatically remember a movie because all its information and all the scenes are in action form.

**B- Big**, the information which is big in size or has a big impact is better remembered by the brain. When you come home from a fair and think about it, the big swings come to your mind first.

**C- Colourful**, the things which are colourful, our brain preserves them better. In newspapers or notebooks, your attention goes more to colourful information than black and white.

**D- Dimensional**, that is, things which are seen in three-dimensional form as tangible objects are remembered easily. For example, there is a word, airplane. On hearing this, the picture of an airplane appears in your mind. Whereas if the word is self-control, then no picture appears immediately.

**E- Emotional**, things which have an emotional impact on the mind are remembered easily. Suppose you have to tell who stood first in the civil services (IAS) this year, then you will not remember it. But if he is your brother, son or friend, you can never forget him because you have an emotional connection with him.

Children, if you use this principle while studying and visualize every information or subject in your mind, then you will remember it easily and firmly and will remember it easily in the exam. The children were very happy to hear about this ABCDE principle and said, Chacha ji, now we will remember the principles of ABCD of childhood very well which will help us in studies and the children clapped a lot after understanding this method of Chacha ji.

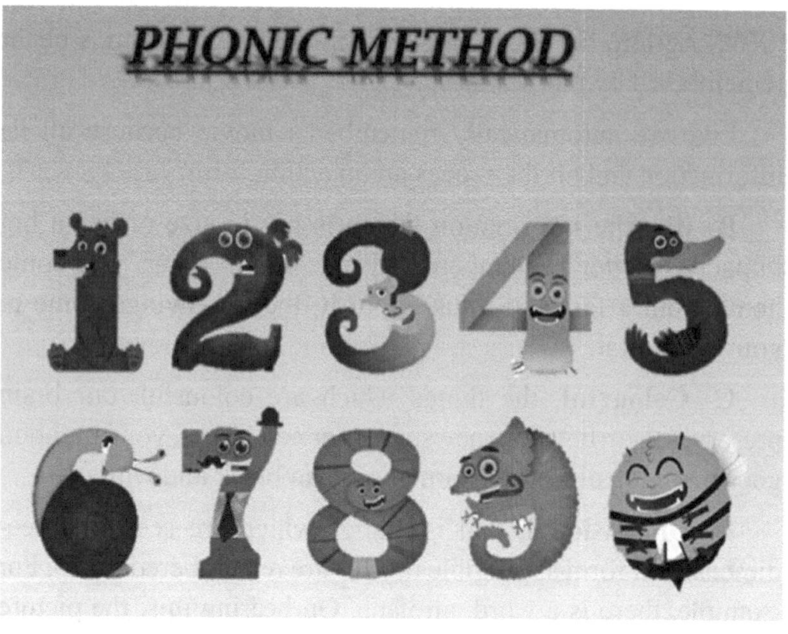

## PHONIC METHOD

## Letter Codes For Digits

| Digit | Letter |
|---|---|
| 0 | S |
| 1 | T, D |
| 2 | n |
| 3 | m |
| 4 | r |
| 5 | L |
| 6 | J, g |
| 7 | K |
| 8 | f, v |
| 9 | P, b |

## Topic 2.22 - How Chacha Chaudhary became a walking clock

The secret of knowledge is his punctuality, Chacha Chaudhary and Sabu were sitting in the morning, where Chacha Chaudhary is trying to remember his daily appointments.

Chacha Chaudhary said, "Sabu, today I have to remember three appointments, and I thought, why not use the brain science Peg System to remember them in a fun way?"

Sabu said, "Chacha ji, I am always ready to help you, so what is the first appointment today?"

Chacha Chaudhary said, "The first appointment is with the dentist at 10 am. Now the code for 10 (TEN) is PEN, so I am imagining myself at the dentist and my teeth are being cleaned with a PEN." (Laughs) "Just think, how weird it would be to clean teeth with a PEN!"

Sabu (laughing), "Yes Chacha ji, that will be really weird."

"Now the next appointment?" Chacha Chaudhary said, "I have to meet Amitabh Bachchan at 12 o'clock. 12 (TWELVE) is code for SHELF so I am imagining Amitabh Bachchan standing on the shelf in my house and saying to me, 'Chacha ji, come, let's talk!"

Saabu said, "I will also be shocked to see Amitabh Bachchan on the shelf!"

Chacha Chaudhary (laughing), "That's the magic of brain science, it becomes easy to remember weird images. Now the third appointment is at 15 o'clock (3:00 pm) in the board office. 15 o'clock (FIFTEEN) is code for LIFTING, so I am seeing myself lifting a heavy board, as if I have to lift a heavy board to go to the office."

Sabu, "Chacha ji, you are amazing. Now I understand that brain science can help in remembering things so easily."

Chacha Chaudhary, "Sabu, this is the fun of Peg System! Exercise your brain and remember everything easily. Now that you are ready for today, shall we go to the dentist?"

Sabu said, "Come on Chacha ji, your day is set today!"

Chacha Chaudhary and Sabu use their brain in their own fun way and easily remember the appointments of the day. Chacha Chaudhary and Sabu are going towards the dentist.

Sabu said, "Chacha ji, this brain science is really very interesting. I think, now I can also use it. But tell me one thing, if more appointments increase, can we remember in the same way?"

Chacha Chaudhary (laughing), "Absolutely, Sabu! As the appointments increase, we can create new mental images. For example, if there is an appointment at 14 o'clock (2 pm), then FOURTEEN is coded for FORT-IN. Now if there is an appointment at 14 o'clock, I can visualize myself standing on the top of the fort and talking to someone."

Sabu (surprised), "Chacha ji, this is very easy! This is all new for me, but even I can imagine it. Another question is – if something has to be remembered for a very long time, is this peg system useful?"

Chacha Chaudhary, "Very good question, Sabu! PEG system is very useful for short term memory, but if we have to remember something for a long time, then we can also use techniques like visualization, storytelling or mind mapping. For example, if we have to remember something after 6 months, then it will be easy to convert it into a story. The brain remembers stories and pictures quickly."

Sabu (understanding), "Oh, so that means the more strange and interesting story we make, the better we can remember?"

Chacha Chaudhary (smiling), "Absolutely! The brain remembers only those things which are unique and fun. If you make even everyday things fun and unique, then the brain cannot forget them." (On reaching the dentist's clinic.)

Sabu, "So Chacha ji, your first appointment started with the cleaning of the pen. Now after this, do you remember the meeting with Amitabh Bachchan on the shelf?"

Chacha Chaudhary (laughing), "Yes, Sabu!"

Sabu said, "Amitabh Bachchan is waiting for you on the shelf, and after that the challenge of lifting the board!

"Today's day has been set in a wonderful way, Chacha ji. Now I will also adopt this method to remember my appointments."

Chacha Chaudhary, "You are right, Sabu! Now we have to work smartly with brain science. We will work hard, but with smartness." Chacha Chaudhary and Sabu spend the day remembering their appointments with ease and having fun, showing that the techniques of brain science not only make things easier but also fun.

Sabu said, "Okay Chacha ji, now a new question has arisen, that is, whatever coding you are telling, like the code for 12, you told the shelf. The code for 10, you told the pen. From where will they know this code. They will also have to remember it."

Chacha ji, "Arre Sabu, it is very simple. It is Numeric Mnemonic Method (NMM)."

In this method, the number is converted into an image. For example, convert numbers from 1 to 20 into images according to their sounds.

Like the similar sounding word for (1) ONE is Gun.

The similar sounding word for (2) TWO is Zoo.

Similarly, (12) TWELVE is Shelf and (10) TEN is Pen.

Did you understand anything, Buddhu Ram? I have told you this before, you might have forgotten. So, just by numeric mnemonics, you can see any number in an image and associate your appointment with that image. It becomes easy, right?

Sabu said, "Yes Chacha ji, I have understood now."

And with this the conversation ended and Chacha ji got busy with his work.

HOLISTIC SUCCESS

Why do some people
Climb mountains?
It's all about...
S.......H......A......K....T.....I

## Topic 2.23- How does Chacha Chaudhary remember the toughest numbers?

Chacha Chaudhary often used to talk to the children of his neighbourhood about their studies. Chacha told the children that today we will tell you about a technique which you would have never heard or read before. The children asked enthusiastically, "What is it, Chacha ji?"

Chacha Chaudhary tells that this technique fits the math numbers in our brain permanently by showing them pictures and we can easily remember the numbers and never forget them. Everyone knows how important is memorizing in exams. But do you know that the time taken to memorize is different for different content. Have you ever noticed how much time it actually takes us to memorize?

Many times, we don't know how much time is required to memorize a topic or chapter firmly and completely. Actually, the time taken to memorize depends on the topic or the type of information.

It is easiest to memorize things that are visible, which have a three-dimensional picture. Like small children are shown things in play-school and they learn by seeing them. It is more difficult to remember words. It is more difficult to remember rhyming subjects like poems. It is more difficult to remember groups of words i.e. sentences, it is more difficult to remember groups of sentences i.e. theories. And the most difficult thing is to remember numbers. Because numbers are abstract.

Actually, in the eyes of the mind, that information is easy to remember which along with its actual meaning, some pictorial information is also visible. Like if I say airplane, then the picture of airplane comes in your mind and its name also and you know its meaning also. If a picture is also given along with the word, then this picture information is auxiliary information which makes the subject simple. But if I say thirty-two, now 32 will come to your mind but no specific picture will come. Since numerical information does not have any auxiliary picture, hence numerical information is confusing and is remembered after a long time by repeating it again and again. Let us know today how numerical information is made. Such numerical information should be given in graphical form.

If I say do you remember which was the first car your father had? You will be able to visualize that car, if I ask do you remember its number? Then many times most of the people get confused. On asking which bank account you have, the bank will start appearing in your mind but you do not remember the bank account number, the names, addresses and faces of friends are remembered but their phone or mobile numbers have to be noted in the phone or diary.

Even in studies, we keep forgetting square root, cube root, mathematical formulas, historical dates, tables, etc. even after repeating them again and again. The reason is that the brain remembers numerical subjects late and forgets them quickly. Because there is no pictorial supporting information with numbers. Let us learn today how to convert numbers into pictorial form.

"This is the brain science Phonetic method," said Chacha ji.

See, these numbers are from zero to nine and all the numbers are formed from these.

Now convert them into English letters in the form of a sound.

Consider zero as 'S', one as 'T', two as 'N', three as 'M', four as 'R', five as 'L', six as 'J', seven as 'K', eight as 'F' and nine as 'P'.

Note that all the letters given to these numbers are consonants, not vowels, because vowels will be used to make words and pictures from these letters. Now let us take an example. For example, to see the 2 and 5 in the pictorial form, take the letters symbolizing the numbers, 2 - N and 5 - L. Now, by adding vowels between N and L, a word can be formed, nail or nala or blue (colour) such pictures can be formed and the symbol of 25, nail or nala will be the supporting picture.

Let us take another example, 32 means 3 and 2. In the phonetic form, 3 means M and 2 means N. By adding vowels to M and N, moon can be formed and it will be visible.

In this way, you can make your own phonetic code for every number and by associating the main information with these pictures, you can remember it.

For example, Article 19C of the Constitution is related to 'freedom of speech'. To remember, 19C means one and nine, phonetic codes are T and P respectively. 'Tape' can be formed by adding vowels. Imagine that you are holding the tap like a microphone and saying whatever you want because there is freedom of speech.

And, this way it will be remembered. And with this method, information containing numbers can make easy pictures. Now you can remember any of your mobile numbers or any maths number.

The children were very happy to hear this, clapped a lot, and said, "Chacha ji, till date no one had taught us the technique of remembering maths numbers. This is a very easy technique. We can remember many things with this which we find difficult in maths. Now it will be easy for us to remember it. By this method, we will give a code and an image to every number and then we can relate it to it and remember it well."

❐

ABC of Brain
Making things ridiculous with ABC
Actionable, BIGGER, Colorful
Let's understand ABC with Tomato

*Chapter - 3*

# Sabu - (SHAKTI - POWER) Everyone has, if they have a brain like Chacha Chaudhary!

Chacha Chaudhary and his Sabu, who always solve even the most difficult tasks with great ease. Chacha Chaudhary's brain works faster than a computer, and Sabu's strength is such that he can even move mountains. But have you ever thought that not only physical strength, but right thinking and brain power can also solve every problem?

## Everyone has power like Sabu

Sabu, who has come from the planet Jupiter, has amazing physical strength, when he gets angry, volcanoes start erupting on Jupiter. But, if we observe, the real power is not in Sabu, but in Chacha Chaudhary's wisdom.

**All of us have 'Sabu' i.e. power in some form or the other. This power can be physical, mental, emotional or spiritual.**

We all are powerful in our respective fields, but many times we are not able to use this power properly. The reason for this is that we lack the wisdom of Chacha Chaudhary.

In fact, Chacha Chaudhary's brain is the real power.

Chacha Chaudhary teaches us that being powerful is not enough, we should also know how to use intelligence. When Sabu is unable to solve a problem with strength, then Chacha Chaudhary uses his cleverness and sharp mind to find a solution. Whether it is to deal with a villain or to find the answer to a difficult puzzle, Chacha Chaudhary proves every time that brain power is the biggest power.

The same thing applies in our lives too. No matter how much power, money or resources we have, if we do not have the ability to think correctly and plan, we can get entangled in even the biggest problems.

Sabu has immense power, but if he uses it without thinking, it can cause harm. The same thing applies to our life too. Whatever power we have, whether it is physical or mental, we should use it in the right direction. We can face the challenges of life not only with strength, but also with patience and wisdom.

Every person has his own 'strength'. It is not necessary that the strength should be physical like Sabu. Some have the power of creative thinking; some have patience and endurance. Every person has some special quality and this is his real strength. If we combine the power of Sabu and the intelligence of Chacha Chaudhary, then no difficulty in life can stop us. It is not enough to have physical strength; we have to develop mental power as well. We have to understand that the real power is within us, we just need to recognize it and use it in the right direction. Every person has that 'Sabu', we just need to recognize it, enlighten it and work in the right direction. If we use our brain properly like Chacha Chaudhary, then we can solve any problem.

The pair of Chacha Chaudhary and Sabu teaches us that the right combination of strength and intelligence is the solution to every problem in life. We all have our own powers, but we should know how to use them in the right direction and at the right time. If we have a mind like Chacha Chaudhary and strength like Sabu, then we can face any challenge in life. There is Sabu (power) in our life too. Every human being wants to achieve success in life and also makes efforts for it, but not everyone gets the desired success.

Look at the sentence below which says, "Why do **some** people climb mountains?"

What is the important word in this, some people will say Parvat, because only when we can see the destination, we will walk, some people will say climbing is important because only if you put effort, you will get success.

I agree but in my view the most important thing is **SOME**, because some people climb, you can also climb, anyone can climb, Parvat is the same, Mount Everest is also the same, so you can also climb, you can also become IAS if you want, you can clear NDA, CDS, you can be successful, you can also be super successful, if you want you can do everything, but only a **few/some** are successful. You can climb Mount Everest, I can also climb it, anyone can climb it, Heller-Tensing climbed it, you can climb it but they don't climb it, some people do what everyone can see, some people achieve that destination, they are one percent people, they have an X factor of success inside them or they generate it.

People have to be passionate and determined, we have to be among such people because exam is not for everyone, it is for some. Many people will apply for it, but few will come to appear in the exam, 8 lakhs will appear, 5 lakhs will appear, all of them are those who can visualize Mount Everest, but only a few people will climb it, you are going to be one of them. Because we will use science, passion, emotions, technology and we will do it in a new way. Don't imagine that if you have modern tools to conquer Mount Everest, your speed will increase 10 times and you will achieve success quickly, but first of all you should have the quality of those **some** people to not leave the field. There are reasons when work is done, there are reasons when it is not done, there are reasons for success and there are reasons for failure. It is like a video game, you clear a level, make mistakes, play again and one day you clear everything. So, you have to play it like a game and visualize yourself a player. I can make you a player, but these few factors will make you a champion.

You will become a champion yourself. I call this **SHAKTI**.

**S - SKILL,**

**H - HABIT,**

**A - ATTITUDE,**

**K - KNOWLEDGE,**

**T - TIME MANAGEMENT,**

**I - INTELLIGENCE.**

The word "SHAKTI" is often associated with power, energy and strength. In the context of personal development, education and life success, "SHAKTI" can be turned into a powerful acronym that represents the formula for achieving success. Each letter of the word "SHAKTI" represents a key element.

It shows that which contributes to overall success- skills, habits, attitude, knowledge, time management and intelligence.

Let us know how each of these components plays an important role in shaping a successful life, especially for students.

Attitude is the first thing that is important for us.

1. **ATTITUDE-** A person's attitude or outlook is the main component of his personality which becomes a factor in his success or failure. Thinking negatively, if there is a negative attitude, the result can never be positive or

successful, whereas with a positive attitude, success is not only natural, but even the impossible can be made possible. This explains the difference between desire and intention. There is a difference between desire and intention. Desire can be bargained but intention cannot be bargained. Whenever there is pressure in life, desires become weak and intentions become strong. You want to become an IAS, you want to clear your government exam, you want to become meritorious, you want to be successful. This should not be your desire. All the people in the world have common desires. Success, happiness, name-fame, money. All the people living in the world have the same desires but not all of them are successful. Only one percent of them is successful because those one percent have the attitude to convert their desires into intentions. So, you should have that attitude. After that, you decide that now I will become an IAS, I have learned it or it was fun, now I will climb the mountain, I will become successful. You have made up your mind, should possess strong attitude. Now, will you climb barefoot? Will you climb without any luggage? Do you have the knowledge of how to climb Everest? You will not be able to climb it, you will fail, you will suffer loss, your time will also be wasted, your life can also be ruined. Hence, after attitude, the second factor is knowledge.

2. **KNOWLEDGE-** The first requirement for doing any work is knowledge. The identity of any successful person in this world is his knowledge in his field of work. ***"Gyanam Manushyasya Tritiyam Netram"*** it is said in the scriptures that with knowledge you can see that which is not visible even with both eyes. What is there on Mars, how is the sun, is it cold in that place,

you have not gone and seen everything, what is there on both our poles, what is happening in which country, you must have read all this, heard about it, have taken knowledge of it, so with knowledge we get the third eye. So, when you study what knowledge will come in the syllabus, which questions will come, how to understand it, what to do, what to learn, what to avoid, this knowledge is necessary for you. For a storehouse of knowledge, you can have a book, you can have YouTube, you can have an application, you can have notes or you can find it somewhere. If you are going to coaching, then the material you get from there can be your knowledge. That is why, to do any work, you must have correct and good knowledge about it. The first and fundamental requirement for success is to have solid and correct knowledge.

3. **HABIT-** But that is not true, nothing will happen by collecting knowledge. Every person in this world has this knowledge, this knowledge that by doing exercise and yoga, the body remains good and healthy, everyone knows. Nothing happens by just having knowledge. Every person knows that smoking cigarette is harmful for health. This knowledge should be written on the cigarette box also. A person knows that fast food is harmful, that is, we have knowledge about what is good and what is bad for our life, still only bad is happening in our life. The reason for this is not only knowledge, but that knowledge will also have to be converted into a habit.

You have got the right knowledge, if you have got the ability then you should have the habit of reading notes daily, revising them, trying new techniques on them, improving your learning, doing daily self-study, if it will be beneficial then habits are the important thing, its formula is 7, 21, 90, 180.

In 7 days, we make up our mind by connecting our desire and intention with knowledge that now we will do this regularly. For example, if you start going for morning walk for the first seven days, then the habit starts developing from the eighth day. After that, if you do it till the 21st day or keep doing it despite all the tiredness, despite all the laziness, then on the 21st day, the habit will be formed. You will not feel tired, you will not feel bad going there and laziness will stop coming in you. If you are studying and your notes are ready, then for the first seven days you have enthusiasm, after that from the eighth day to the 21st day, you start feeling lazy and you develop a tendency to postpone work. Generally, I have seen this problem in 90% of the experts I have seen. You remain full of enthusiasm for 7 days and after that from the eighth day onwards that motivation goes down. If you maintain that enthusiasm and motivation from the seventh day to the 21st day then from the 22nd day onwards you should do self-meditation for 2-3 hours or 5 hours. You will not feel bad about doing self-study. You will get a comfort factor in it. That means it will form a habit. Knowledge does not help and when that habit is formed, if you keep doing it for 90 days, it will become a skill. Then you will start enjoying it. Then you will enjoy reading four books in a month. Your reading speed will become very good. Your writing speed will become good. You will understand the notes. Four pages of a book will tell you whether the book is written by a good writer or not. Should I study or not? This interest will develop. This skill will make you a good reader, a good student, a friend. A reading champion will be born inside you and if you do that for 6 months, then you cannot live without it. That is, if you have connected your knowledge with your habit for 180 days, then after 6 months you will not be able to tolerate that you are not studying for

5 hours. You will not be able to tolerate that you are not doing self-study. That is, a permanent champion will reside inside you. Your exam will be waiting for you and you will be waiting for the exam. You will already know what the result is going to be.

4. **SKILL-** Knowledge of any work is necessary to do it but to reach the top position in that work and to make a name for yourself, it is necessary to be skilled in it. Skill comes from continuous practice of knowledge and determination gives you the strength to face the challenges and win. When you learn to drive a car, you acquire the technical knowledge on the very first day, but the skill in driving comes from continuous practice and only then you can drive the car easily. This is applicable in every field. In studies also, along with knowledge, skill shows the way to success.
5. **TIME MANAGEMENT-** When you have skill, then the time which was taking earlier, gets managed, like what you do in the whole day these days, you know how mummy does it in 15 minutes in the morning. You will cook food in 1 hour, clothes will be done within 1 hour, the house will be set by 9 o'clock. So, this time is managed. So, when you convert your studies into time management, that is, you will learn to manage yourself at the time of your studies, then a champion will arise inside you, which you will see then, you will know that this can be done in 18 days. I will complete it in 25 days. If there are 10,000 questions, I will complete it in two months. Time is everything. If you have controlled your time, managed it or become a time manager, then you have become successful. You will become the manager of your life. Then, what would take 10 hours, will take 5 hours. If you apply science in those 5 hours, then it

will take two hours or one hour. Time management is done. When you become skilled in driving a car, then a distance of 100 kms which is covered in two days by walking, can be covered in two hours by car. Because you have become skilled, then time management can be done. Then you will know that you have to go and come back in less time. And if you want to do a work in less time, according to your time, as per your wish. If you can do this then you are intelligent.

6. **INTELLIGENCE-** Intelligence is the ability to learn, understand and apply knowledge. But it is not just about what you know. It is also about how you use what you know to solve problems and adapt to new situations. Intelligence can be developed and increased through practice, curiosity, willingness to learn from mistakes. You become intelligent and you develop intelligence in yourself. All the successful people in this world, who are doing business, are officers, politicians, Prime Minister of the country or any other big writer, Bollywood celebrity, anyone who is super successful, very few people are super successful.

   There are people who are super successful, one thing is common in all of them, all intelligent people have the power to control their mind, this is the difference between knowledge and intelligence. The power to speak is knowledge, ability to speak is knowledge but ability to listen is intelligence. But the power to listen and understand is wisdom, intelligence. If you understand this power, then you also become like Chacha Chaudhary who has a powerful saabu. So, remember, everyone has 'Sabu', you just need to have a brain like Chacha Chaudhary!

### Topic 3.1 - Who is the real VIP??

One day Chacha Chaudhary was sitting in the garden outside his house, when Chachi ji started discussing about children and parents. Sabu and Rocket, sitting nearby, were also listening attentively. Chachi ji asked, "Tell me, nowadays everyone wants to become a VIP, but who is a real VIP?"

Chacha Chaudhary smiled and said, "Nowadays people run after becoming VIPs, but actually if you are intelligent, then you automatically become important. Only those people who are intelligent are respected in the society."

Chachi ji asked in surprise, "Does intelligence mean only being good in studies?"

Chacha Chaudhary laughed and said, "No, intelligence means the ability to take the right decisions, to understand every situation and work accordingly. Like the parents who guide their children in the right direction are actually VIPs."

Sabu asked curiously, "Chacha ji, if someone wants to become an intelligent parent, what should he do?"

Chacha Chaudhary explained seriously, "To become a VIP parent, you have to have faith in the ability of your children. Every child has something special; you just have to recognize it."

VERY INTELLIGENT PARENTS

VIP

INDIA

Then he told eight important things that every parent should keep in mind:

1. **Trust-** Have faith in children and build a trusting relationship with them.
2. **Be a good listener-** Listen to children carefully and try to understand them.
3. **Give time-** Spending time with children is their emotional and mental need.
4. **Motivate-** Instead of pressurizing them, motivate them and develop their abilities.
5. **Develop the whole personality-** Don't just run after marks, focus on their overall development.
6. **Give healthy food-** Good and nutritious food is necessary for the physical and mental development of children.
7. **Be a friend-** Be a true friend of your children so that they can share their inner feelings with you.
8. **Encourage specialties-** Recognize and encourage the qualities that the child has.

On hearing this, Chachi ji said, "So this means that if we don't take care of these things, then we can also become VIP parents?"

Chacha Chaudhary smiled and said, "Of course, when children move in the right direction, they will automatically become important. And if parents are intelligent, then children will also become intelligent. This is the secret of becoming a real VIP."

Sabu and Rocket clapped on hearing this, and Chachi ji said proudly, "Looks like I have already steered Sabu in the right direction. Now I will have to explain to the rest of the world that the real VIPs are those who become intelligent parents."

Thus, Chacha Chaudhary explained that intelligence and right upbringing are the only ways to become a real VIP in the society.

## Topic 3.2- Values for Success in Life- Importance of Values

Chachi Ji asked Chacha Ji- "Tell me the difference between clever and intelligent."

Chacha Ji said, "There are two types of people in the world, one is simple and the other is those who have sharp mind, in the second type of people also there are two types of people, one clever and the other intelligent, the first difference between clever and intelligent is their values. A clever person is a threat to the society and an intelligent person is the need of the society. One similarity between clever and intelligent people is that both have sharp brains, they know how to use their brains in the best possible way. For example, it is like a terrorist and a security officer, both are proficient in using weapons. The common thing between both is that both are sharp fighters, both have expertise in using weapons, but a terrorist is a threat to us and he is a clever person, whereas a security officer is an intelligent person who is needed by our society. But the similarity between both is that both have sharp brains. Our police commissioner and dacoit Gobar Singh, both have sharp brains, but commissioner is needed by the society and dacoit Gobar Singh or Raka is a threat to the society.

If a person has a sharp mind with values and ethics, then only he is intelligent, he is wise, but if he does not have values and ethics with a sharp mind, then that person is a clever person, he uses things for his own selfishness even if it causes a little harm to others, an intelligent person uses his mind for the benefit of others and for the development of society.

Intelligent people are needed in society, just like a gem gets importance when it passes through the grindstone of a jeweller like a precious stone, then it becomes an ornament, a jewellery, a precious gem. Gold too has value only when it is heated, forged or made into jewellery and only then it becomes a gem. Similarly, a sharp mind and knowledge will have value only when it is accompanied by values, morality, character, Sanskar and integrity. Unless a man undergoes this process, his sharp mind and knowledge will have no value and will not be of any use to the society and the nation, no matter how sharp his mind is. When ethics and character are established in us, it will give moral merit to our character, it will adorn the abilities and skills that are within you, it will give it form and shape. There are many types of values: -

1. **Academic value-** When you score good marks in the exam, your studies should not be just rote learning, you should know the importance of doing it, what is the use of whatever I have studied in life, what is its use in building my personality, academic value includes reading, writing, understanding, finding out its usefulness in your life, studying its philosophy, science and in every way, and then establishing it, for this, using many methods like brain science, etc., by doing all this your academic value is established, along with scoring good marks, you can also learn to use knowledge in life. You should also know the importance of education, only then it will benefit you in life. You should know what is its use in life, along with that you should know what is useful for your personality development and also establish it in a good way. The value of academics should not only be in the getting good marks in mark sheets, but also in the development of personality and intelligence.

2. **Moral Values-** What is integrity and honesty, is there any difference between them, or are honesty and loyalty the same - honesty is not doing wrong things. Some people do not do wrong things because they do not want to be caught doing wrong things, they are doing the right thing but for the wrong reason. That is, if you are assured that you will never be caught, then you will start doing wrong things, that is, you are doing the right thing but for the wrong reason. But if a person comes to know that no one is watching him, and he will not be caught, still he will not do wrong things, only then he is truly honest, he is doing the right thing because he knows that it is right and he is not doing wrong because he believes that this work is wrong and I will not do it.

   Doing the right thing for the right reason is loyalty which is above being honest. There should be honesty in your character as well as loyalty. People with loyalty do not do wrong things because they know that they should not do wrong things and they will not do wrong even if no one in the world is watching them. You must have seen examples in our society that sometimes someone's bag got lost and a person searched for the person who owned it and returned the bag to him, he suffered for that, still he searched for it from anywhere and returned it.

   They delivered it to him because they know that they will do good and right work, they will not keep someone else's property for themselves but will also deliver it to the right owner. They will never do wrong but will stand with the right. They have character and values. If seen, they are the wealth of our society, assets for our society.

3. **Time Management Value-** If there is any real wealth in life, then it is time. If time is spent, then it will never be

recovered. Even a moment cannot be regained. If you learn to manage time, then life will be managed automatically. If you look at any loss in life properly, then in reality it is a loss of time only. In this universe, every person has got comforts, wealth and things in different quantities in his life. Everyone has different things and in different quantities. Some are rich and some are poor. Some have a car and some have a bullock cart. Somewhere only one person lives in a big bungalow and somewhere the whole family lives in a small hut. Some have full groceries and someone is not able to get two meals a day. Someone has a lot of knowledge and someone is illiterate. That means every person has different things from the other and in different quantities. But one thing is equally available to everyone and that too in exactly the same quantity, that is time. Every person has 24 hours in a day, everyone has a 7-day week, everyone has equal number of months and years. That means everyone has equal amount of time without any bias. Some get everything by using this time properly, become successful, and some lose everything by misusing time, get ruined.

The one who learns to value time is successful. Time tells the losers that- Yesterday you destroyed me, today I am destroying you, all is equal. Time is always equal, all is equal. Doing every work with discipline and achieving mastery in it is the real time management, by which we learn to save time, by mastery means skill, we learn to do any work in less time, the work in which we have mastery takes less time to do and time is saved. This is the basic mantra of being successful.

4. **Learning value-** Learning means learning or becoming skilled. Learning is more important than knowing and

understanding. For example, in studies, one should complete the learning cycle and convert one's academic value into learning. Reading, writing, understanding, memorization, retention are the first five inputs and recollection is the output. And in exams, only the output is important. Efforts are appreciated but results are rewarded! But recollection should be converted into learning and knowledge should not remain in your mind only till the exam but throughout life. That knowledge should be converted into a skill. Also, Knowledge is appreciated but only Skills are rewarded!! And there should be the right knowledge and should be based on the right values, i.e. knowledge should be in the right direction and should be based on values only then the right skill will develop. Just acquiring knowledge or being proficient in some work is not enough for that. For that, ethics and values are also necessary. Learning means to convert knowledge into correct skills. Only through real learning, learners are formed who are needed by the society and help in building a better society. Any knowledge may be obtained from schools or from parents or teachers or from any environment but that knowledge should have values. It should be in the right direction so that a good society and a good country can be built. A person can be intelligent as well as a good citizen. Knowledge alone can be beneficial as well as harmful but if knowledge has ethics or values then that knowledge gives birth to a correct skill and a correct culture. Just like medicines are made from chemistry and drugs are also made from chemistry. Medicines save lives and drugs take lives and ruin lives. These drugs have pushed our youth towards destruction. Those who make drugs are benefiting themselves and spreading destruction in the rest of the world. That is, the basis of whatever work you do is that it should have values and ethics, it should have the right learning and right knowledge. It is dangerous to have too much knowledge without values. People say that people need efficiency or skill or competency. But the truth is that efficiency or skill or combativity or knowledge without values is dangerous. Without values, it is a danger. If the gun is in the hands of a criminal, then his skill of using the gun will become a threat to the society or any person and if the same gun is in the hands of a soldier or a police officer, then a sense of security will come. The gun is the same, the skill of using it is also the same but the policeman has policies, the policeman has rules. He knows which way to use it, which way to use to prevent crime and where not to use it to protect people, only these policies should be established as a learning value.

Sabu is so powerful, suppose if Sabu becomes a bad person, then it will be a big mess that he will become dangerous, even thinking that he seems dangerous, but because of Chacha Chaudhary, Sabu also remains a good person and good works are done in the whole society and country, with his understanding and power, he does good work in the world and becomes the pride of the society and the country.

This is the meaning of learning values that it is necessary to be with learning values.

Chachi ji asked Chacha ji, tell something for the children, Chacha ji, how to inculcate values in your life:

Chacha ji says, these rules that I am telling you, they have to be followed so that they can inculcate the importance of value for success in their life - General Values.

**Positive thinking-** Always think about how to be successful and always stay positive. Whatever the subject or exam, do not be afraid of it, nor get stressed. Rather tell yourself that nothing is beyond your mind and intention. Never think that it is difficult and will not happen. Rather say that it is easy and will definitely happen. Never think in stress that the problem is not a problem but a riddle or puzzle. It is fun to solve these puzzles. If you think like this, then the problems of life will also be solved. You will also enjoy solving them.

**Time management-** Organize and manage your activities and tasks through time management. Divide your time into parts and decide your routine. Divide your time into two parts, urgent and important. Keep the things which are less important but not urgent on the second rung and give the first priority to the things which are urgent. For example, if you have received an electricity bill at your home and the due date is after 15 days, then this work is important but not urgent. Whereas on the last day, this work will become important as well as urgent.

**Effective study-** Study not just to score marks but to learn and gain knowledge. Build an emotional connection with the subject. Create interest in it. Treat it not just as a subject but as a skill in life. Learn that just like you use Facebook, Internet, WhatsApp not for getting marks but for knowledge out of interest, we read newspaper not for getting marks but for living and for information, similarly take your subject and concentrate on its knowledge as well as its usefulness in life.

**Read at intervals-** Just as we cannot eat the whole day's food at once, we have to eat it at different intervals, similarly instead of studying continuously, take a rest of 10 to 15 minutes after every hour of study, this makes learning permanent and the brain gets full energy.

**Good sleep-** Good and complete sleep keeps your brain organized and energetic. Take 8 hours of sleep, do not go and study at night, rather study your syllabus according to time management and just sleep at night.

**Innovative-** Always think of doing something new, keep new information about a subject and remain curious

**Good food-** Always eat good and healthy food. Avoid fast food and market food. Drink fruit juices and eat salads a lot. Drink lots of water. Water keeps your body and mind fresh and healthy. Do meditation and exercise. Students should remain healthy in both mind and body. For this, they should sleep early and wake up early. Do some exercise regularly and definitely do meditation. This keeps the mind, brain and body healthy. It makes you energetic and strong, thus concentration increases.

**Plan the exam properly-** Keep the important questions and topics firmly fixed in time, wherever there is doubt, do not hesitate to ask your teachers for help in re-understanding the topic. Make a target that how many syllabuses are there, how many marks are to be scored and how to complete them.

**Focus on one topic at a time-** Instead of studying everything, keep one question or topic in focus and complete it at a time. Do not think that there is so much topic, which question will come in this syllabus and which will not, think that if this question comes then it will be absolutely correct.

## Topic 3.3 - Chacha Chaudhary's wisdom: How to avoid mistakes in exams and life!

Chacha Chaudhary's wisdom: How to avoid mistakes in exams and life!

The time of examinations was coming near and the children of the village were getting nervous. Everyone was thinking, "If only we could score good marks without making mistakes." But mistakes are a part of life, and it is always difficult to avoid them in exams.

Then Chacha Chaudhary, whose brain works faster than a computer, gathered the children and said, "Everyone makes mistakes, but how to avoid those mistakes is an art. Today I will tell you some easy ways, which will reduce your mistakes not only in exams but also in life." Sabu, who could move mountains with his strength, also smiled and said, "If you have self-confidence like me and intelligence like Chacha ji, then there is no question of mistakes!"

Chhotu said, "Chacha ji, I make a lot of mistakes in exams. You tell me, what should I do?"

Chacha Chaudhary stroked his moustache and said smilingly, "Chhotu, there is no need to worry. It is easy to avoid mistakes in exams and life, if you follow some of my advice."

Chhotu asked curiously, "Which advice, Chacha ji?"

### First: Keep your Focus (Concentration)

Chacha Chaudhary said, "Look, Chhotu, what will happen if your attention wanders to uncle's sweet shop during exams?" Chhotu scratched his head and said, "Then I will remember the *jalebis* and make mistakes."

Chacha ji said, "Absolutely! That is why whenever you are studying or taking an exam, just concentrate on studying. Everything else comes later!"

### Second: Time management

Chacha Chaudhary took out his watch from his pocket and said, "Proper use of time is important, otherwise your condition will become like Sabu's!"

Sabu asked in surprise, "Me? What did I do?"

Chacha said, "Your habit of sleeping on time made you lose every wrestling match."

Chhotu said laughingly, "I understood Chacha ji, now I will also divide my time for studies!"

## Third: Answer with understanding

Chacha Chaudhary asked Chhotu a question, "Tell me, if a cow had two legs, how would it walk?"

Chhotu said laughingly, "Chacha ji, a cow has four legs!"

Chacha shook his head and said, "Absolutely right. Even in exams, first understand the question, then answer, so that you do not make any mistakes!"

## Fourth: Learn from mistakes

Chacha Chaudhary said, "Mistakes will happen, Chhotu, this is certain. But instead of being afraid of them, learn from them, like Sabu loses wrestling every time but learns something new every time. Isn't it, Sabu?" Sabu shook his head smilingly, "Yes, Chacha ji, now I am not afraid of losing ever!"

## Fifth: Skill

Chacha Chaudhary said, "Not only knowledge, skill is also important. If you do not have the right skill, then mistakes are bound to happen in the exam. Like Sabu does not know how to cook, but when it comes to wrestling, his skill is unmatched. Skill i.e. practice is also necessary for the exam."

Sabu said laughingly, "Yes, I can burn food, but no one can defeat me in wrestling!"

## Sixth: Attitude

Chacha Chaudhary explained to Chhotu, "The right attitude is also important. If you go to the exam with a negative attitude, then you will lose in the first place. Have a positive attitude, like I solve every problem by considering it an opportunity." Chhotu said, "I understood, Chacha ji! From now on I will prepare with a positive attitude."

## Seventh: Habit

Chacha Choudhary said, "Chhotu, your habits create your future. Like Sabu has a habit of getting up early in the morning and exercising, that is why he is always strong. You should also develop a good habit of studying, so that you never have to worry about the exam."

Chhotu said, nodding his head, "You are right, Chacha ji! From now on I will develop a habit of studying daily."

## Eighth: Don't say 'I wish'!

Chacha Chaudhary gave the last lesson to Chhotu and said, "And the most important thing! Don't make a habit of saying 'I wish'. Whatever work you have to do, do it with full faith and hard work. Instead of 'I wish', think that you will definitely succeed!"

Sabu said laughingly, "Instead of 'I wish', say 'I can do it', only then even the mountain will look small!"

Chhotu listened carefully to Chacha Chaudhary and Sabu and said, "Chacha ji, now I will not say 'I wish', but will prepare for the exam with hard work and knowledge!"

Chacha Chaudhary said smilingly, "Of course, Chhotu!"

"And remember, Chacha Chaudhary's intelligence works faster than a computer, but everyone can learn the cleverness of avoiding mistakes!" Sabu said laughingly, "And yes, if he still makes a mistake, then push him away by becoming strong like me!", ha ha ha and listening to Sabu's words all the children burst out laughing.

## Topic 3.4 - The Secret of Chacha Chaudhary's Knowledge - What to Read - What Not to Read

The Secret of Chacha Chaudhary's Knowledge

One day Chacha Chaudhary and Sabu were sitting under the shed of a tree, when Pinki and Rakesh came running to them. Pinki said, "Chacha ji, we are very confused! There are so many subjects and so much information, we are not able to understand what to study and what not to."

Rakesh also said worriedly, "Yes chacha ji, we are preparing for the exam, but every time something or the other is studied which does not come in the exam."

Chacha Chaudhary smiled and said, "This problem is not only yours, children. Often, we are taught what is not necessary. That is why it is important to understand what should be learned and what should not? Chacha Chaudhary explained, "First of all you have to see what is part of the study and what is not. Not every information is necessary, that is why first of all you have to understand what kind of questions come in the exam." Chacha ji told, "Suppose, there is a chapter in mathematics in which very long definitions have been given, but when you look at the old question papers, you will find that there are only questions based on formulas. So instead of long notes, you should focus on those important formulas."

Sabu scratched his head and asked, "So this means we don't need to memorize everything?"

Chacha ji replied, "Absolutely right! There is no need to memorize everything. Always focus on the important points and questions."

### Importance of Simplification

Chacha Choudhary further said, "Now that you have understood what to study, the next step is to simplify it. Whenever you read a long text, take out the main words from it and leave the rest of the filler words. This will make your reading easier. We call it the Simplification Method."

Pinki asked curiously, "Chacha ji, what is this Simplification Method?"

Chacha ji explained, "Suppose, you have a long chapter of history, which talks about Ashoka the Great. Instead of memorizing the entire story, you can just remember the key words like – 'Ashoka', 'Kalinga War', 'Dhamma', 'Buddhism'. This will make your answer short and precise."

"If you are asked in the exam why Ashoka adopted Buddhism, then you don't need to tell the entire story. You can just tell – 'After the Kalinga War, Ashoka experienced the horrors of war and adopted Buddhism.' This way your answer will be simple and precise."

Sabu said, "Wow! This is a fun way. So, we have to remember only the main points?"

Chacha Choudhary said laughingly, "Absolutely! And this will save your time and also deepen your understanding."

## Identifying questions:

Chacha Chaudhary further said, "When you are preparing for the exam, do not forget to look at the old question papers. This will tell you what kind of questions are asked again and again. Sometimes the same questions are asked in different ways. If you identify them, half the problem will be solved.

"Suppose, there is a science exam. You looked at the previous year's papers and found that every year a question on the change in light comes, even though the form of the question has changed. Now you know that you have to pay special attention to this topic."

Rakesh said in surprise, "Oh yes! We had not thought of this. Looking at old papers can help us a lot."

Chacha ji shook his head and said, "Absolutely! From old question papers you can also know which questions come repeatedly from which subject. This will help you manage your time properly and make your preparation precise."

Finally, Chacha Chaudhary said, "Remember, there is no need to learn everything. You just read those things which are important for the exam. Use your time properly, make things simple, and identify the right questions from old question papers. This will make your studies easy and you will move towards success."

Pinki and Rakesh said excitedly, "Thank you, Chacha ji! Now we know what to study and what not to study."

Chacha Chaudhary smiled and said, "Don't forget that extraordinary success is achieved through ordinary methods."

❒

*Chapter - 4*

# Raka (Challenges) Never dies, Sabu is never afraid of challenges

There used to be Raaka in Chacha Chaudhary's comics, a ruthless villain, His specialty was that he had drunk such a medicine that he did not die.

Many times, he had encounters with Chacha ji and Sabu, every time Chacha ji was successful in stopping him and would defeat him and even drive him away, but then someday he would come again. He kept coming in their life and Chacha Chaudhary and Sabu kept defeating him. They were never afraid of Raaka.

Raka of our life is our problems and challenges which never end completely, as long as there is life, there is some problem or the other, some challenge or the other. These will never end like Raka, but they can be fought and won like Chacha Chaudhary.

If we also become fearless like Sabu and think like Chacha Chaudhary, use our mind like him, do not fear the problems but face them boldly with understanding, then the problems will keep on losing to us. And the more we keep on winning the problems, the more we will move ahead, the more we will improve, the more successful we will become. The people who are more successful in this world are those who have faced more challenges.

## Topic 4.1- Accepting challenges with enthusiasm

From Chacha Chaudhary's life, we can learn that he used to handle challenges and problems in his life with enthusiasm. The biggest thing to learn from Chacha Chaudhary is that whatever difficulties or problems there were in life, whatever bad arrangements there were, he used to enjoy them and solve them. Now how did this mindset come? For this, it is important for us to understand that when any situation comes in front of us in our life, then there are two types of reactions to it - uncontrolled and uncontrolled. This shows that the situations in life are not in our control, but what our reaction is for it is in our control.

We cannot stop problems and difficulties from coming in life, but there are many situations in which we can think primitively and anticipate the challenges and problems and have a solution for them in advance. We cannot stop how we will react to the challenges and problems, however if you have good control over your mind then you can anticipate these challenges in advance. When an airplane is made, some things are kept in mind like it should never crash or there should be no problem in it, so all these problems are thought about in advance and the airplane is made by thinking about its solutions. It is made with the mindset that there should be no problem while flying and while coming back down and everything should be done in a 100% safe manner. But keeping all this in mind, it is also kept in mind that sometimes some one percent situations can come in which things are not in our control and with this thinking a parachute was also made. So here with positive thinking an airplane is made and with positive thinking a parachute is made.

So, this balance comes with an intelligent mindset. That is, it means not letting any problem come or if it has come then finding a solution to it. Similarly, life is also determined by the situation and what is our reaction in that situation. So, problems and challenges come everywhere in life but the question is whether we can solve it like a video game?

Sabu saw that Chacha Chaudhary was playing a video game, so he asked him for that video game for a while and started playing. While playing, Sabu asked Chacha Chaudhary that why do you play this game when it is so difficult? Play some easy game. So, Chacha Chaudhary said that other games are very easy and I do not enjoy them without challenges. When Sabu asked why, Chacha Chaudhary said that there is no fun in doing anything until difficulties come in front. From this we learn that in life when we are doing some work and it starts to seem easy to us, then we start enjoying it and like video games, as soon as we move forward and face challenges and problems, then while solving them we start enjoying life. This is because just like in video games, when we move ahead and new challenges come in front of us, then we start enjoying in overcoming them.

Similarly, when we face challenges in life, when we move ahead after overcoming one challenge, then we start enjoying in solving the other challenges as well. This also shows a positive attitude. This positive thinking and self-confidence make us enjoy overcoming challenges in video games, but why is it that when we face challenges in life, we get nervous? This is because we are not able to keep that self-confidence and positive thinking in life. Chacha Chaudhary teaches us that you have to do two things. In this context, there is a lesson named Shakti, through which you have to learn to become artful and intelligent. And secondly, you have to keep your mentality like a puzzle, that whatever problem is coming in life, you have to see it in a positive way, whether we consider it a problem or a puzzle. If we consider it a problem or a problem, then there will be tension and anxiety and if we consider it the first, then our brain will start working. Whenever we face any problem, our brain can react in two ways, first- this work is very difficult, I will not be able to do it and second- this work is very difficult and how will it be done. In both these situations and both these reactions, there is a feeling of surrender in which we think beforehand that I will not be able to do it and our mind also stops thinking of any suggestion believing this and in such a situation our tension and troubles increase further. And we accept defeat in front of challenges.

The second reaction is that it is difficult but we try to find out how it will be done and how its solution will be found. This shows a positive and suggestive mindset. In this reaction, we accept that yes, this thing is difficult and not easy but we also believe that there is a solution to it and believing this our mind starts working on it. Similarly, in the first situation our brain stops working because we say that this will not happen and in the second situation our brain starts working and starts finding a solution because we ask how it will happen. Chacha Chaudhary's brain works in the same way that when a situation arises, he does not say that this work is difficult but he says that this work can be difficult.

But let's find out how this will be done and his mind starts working and he moves towards the solution. This teaches us that challenges in life, problems should be understood like a video game and should be played like a video game and process should be done towards its solution. In Chacha Chaudhary's life too, many challenges came from small to big and from Gobar Singh to Raja, but Chacha Chaudhary solved every problem and, in the end, enjoying that whole reaction, he stood in front of the challenges as Aladdin and in front of the problems as a problem and showed that he has a solution to every problem in his mind. What are problems afraid of? Problems are afraid of suggestions.

When you stand in front of problems with a positive attitude, then every kind of challenge will be delayed. Chacha

Chaudhary teaches this in life that there are two types of situations in the life of all elders, children and parents, one which you like and one which you do not like. The situation which we do not like can come because we are making mistakes and we are working without thinking about the situations that may come in the future. For this, the lesson named Shakti given in this book will help you from which you can learn how to gain knowledge and become intelligent and skilful. Before doing any work, if we think about what problems or challenges can come in it and if we think about them and find their solution beforehand, then our challenges will seem very easy to us. And if ever such a problem comes about which you are not able to think, then instead of getting scared of it, we should think that no matter how big the problem is, it is still small in front of our imagination and our intentions and we should start thinking about its solution.

Problems arise in the world, when problems are born, their solutions are also born at the same time. When we keep looking for a problem, we see a problem in it, but when we try to find a solution to it, we start seeing a solution. The mind is the fabric of our life. We will not get anything in life on our own, nor does anything happen on its own, rather we have to find it. So, if your focus is on the problem, you will find more problems, but if your focus is on the solution to the problem, you will definitely find a solution to every problem and in this way, you will be able to face all challenges with enthusiasm. It is necessary to identify the difficult and the easy.

For example, what we know seems easy and what we do not know seems difficult. So, when we believe that we know something or we can learn something, then all difficult tasks seem easy to us and as soon as the task becomes easy, we start finding it interesting. And if we start having the mindset that, where will we reach after eliminating all kinds of problems, then we will start seeing a reward in the solution of every problem and we will get enthusiasm in solving that problem.

Similarly, if you develop a positive mindset like Chacha Chaudhary, then you will start facing all the challenges with enthusiasm while enjoying life. For example, in the beginning we find it difficult to make roti, but when we try to make it three or four times, it always seems difficult. When we learn to play harmony, we find it difficult, but when we practice it, we start enjoying it and it starts seeming easy to us. Similarly, the things that we find difficult in the beginning start seeming easy with practice and we start enjoying it. In life, 95% of the challenges do not come to trouble us or break us, but to make us better and to make us more skilled.

For example, in the video game when we fail at a level, we try it again and again and master it and, in this way, we gradually cross all the levels. That game remains the same but we fight its challenges and gain skills in it and make ourselves better. Similarly, in life too, problems are neither small nor big. They remain the same. We become more skilled in them.

## Topic 4.2- Chacha Chaudhary's unique treatment: Drive away stress and fear

One day, strange incidents started happening in the village. Children and adults were all troubled by some kind of stress and phobia. Some were afraid of heights, while others would get drenched in sweat on hearing the name of exams. People were so worried that they had forgotten to laugh and smile. The villagers went to Chacha Chaudhary to get rid of this problem.

Sabu was also sitting there, and Chacha ji's wife was cooking food. The villagers said, "Chacha ji, now the situation has become worse. Our stress and fear never end!"

Chacha Chaudhary smiled and said, "Hey friends, it is not difficult to eliminate stress and fear. Its solution is hidden in our mind itself. Do you know that our brain is divided into two parts – right brain and left brain. Only by balancing these two can we eliminate stress and fear."

Chhotu asked in surprise, "Chacha ji, what is this right and left brain?"

Chacha Chaudhary explained, "Our brain has two parts. The left brain is related to logic, calculation, and analysis. This part helps us to think logically and solve problems. On the other hand, the right brain is associated with our imagination, creativity, and emotions. When we use these two parts of our brain properly, stress and fear go away automatically."

Sabu said in surprise, "Wow Chacha Ji! So is this a brain game? Please tell me how we can use it."

**Chacha Chaudhary's Brain Balancing Technique**

Chacha Chaudhary told the children and villagers a unique way to balance the right and left brain. He said, "Come, I will teach you the brain balancing technique. This will keep your mind absolutely calm and you will not be afraid."

## First: Using the Left Brain (Problem Solving)

Chacha Choudhary said, "If you are struggling with a problem, like a difficult math question or a problem in life, then you should use your left brain. This means that you think logically, understand the information well, and find a solution by analysing it."

Chhotu said, "But Chacha ji, what if we are afraid?"

Chacha Choudhary smiled and said, "To eliminate fear, we have to take the help of the right brain."

## Second: Using the Right Brain (Creativity and Visualization)

Chacha Choudhary explained, “If you ever feel afraid, then use your imagination. The right brain is connected to your creativity and emotions. Whenever you feel scared, close your eyes and imagine a beautiful place. Like walking in the mountains, sitting by a calm lake, or flying in the sky. This technique will calm your mind and eliminate fear.”

Sabu said, “Oh wow! I always use my right brain when I get angry. I imagine myself in a calm place when I am angry.”

## Third: Brain Exercise

Chacha Chaudhary suggested another interesting solution. He said, “If you want to strengthen both the parts together, do some special brain exercises. Like playing crosswords or Sudoku, drawing pictures, or listening to music. This will keep your brain balanced and healthy.”

Pinki asked curiously, “Chacha ji, will this also reduce stress?”

Chacha Chaudhary shook his head and said, “Absolutely! Stress comes when there is imbalance in the brain. If you keep both the parts of your brain strong, not only will your creativity increase, but your reasoning power will also be sharp, and stress will disappear.”

## Fourth: Meditation and deep breathing

Chacha Chaudhary told the last and the easiest method, “If you suddenly feel stressed, take some deep breaths and meditate. This method will immediately calm your mind and balance both the parts of your brain. This will give you mental peace and the fear will go away.”

In a few days, by following the techniques given by Chacha Chaudhary, all the people of the village got rid of their stress and fear. They brought balance in their lives and started dealing with every problem happily.

Sabu said, "Now whenever I am stuck in a problem, I use my left brain to find a solution and if I am scared, I get lost in the imaginations of my right brain. Really, the brain plays an amazing game!"

Chacha Chaudhary said laughingly, "Remember, to get rid of stress and fear in life, learn to use your brain properly. Your brain is your biggest friend and when you use both its parts properly, no problem can scare you."

## Topic 4.3 - Chacha Chaudhary and the journey from confusion to self-confidence

One day, all the children were preparing for the exam in the village school. But Pinki, Chhotu and Rakesh were worried. They were confused and worried which was clearly visible on their faces. They kept opening and closing the books again and again, but were not able to understand anything.

When Sabu saw the children worried, he took them to Chacha Chaudhary.

Pinki said, "Chacha ji, we are very confused. We are not able to understand what we have studied, and the more we study, the more our fear and tension increases. How will we succeed in the exam?"

Chacha Chaudhary smiled and said, "Children, to deal with every problem in exams or life, not only information is needed, but also self-confidence. To overcome confusion, you need proper guidance and a little patience."

Chhotu asked, "Chacha ji, but how to bring about this self-breath?"

Chacha ji said, "The best way to inhale soulful breath is understanding, practice, and self-power. The more deeply you understand, the more you practice, the stronger your self-breathing will become."

Then Chacha Chaudhary said a Sanskrit verse:-

*"Vidya dadati vinyam, vinyad yaati paatrtam*
*Paatravtat dhanmapnoti, dhanat dharma tat sukham."*

Eligibility is the measure of wealth, wealth is religion, wealth is happiness.

It means: *Vidya* (knowledge) comes from *Vinaya* (humility), from Vinaya ability, ability leads to wealth, and wealth leads to religion and happiness, that means knowledge can get rid of all your problems, All the problems of life can be solved by knowledge, just need to utilise it effectively.

Then Chacha Chaudhary taught the children some ways to increase self-confidence:-

## 1. Understanding and clarity

Chacha ji explained, "First of all, to study or do any work, you have to understand it well. Just memorizing without understanding increases confusion. Whatever you are studying, know its meaning and write it in your own words. This will make the subject clear."

## 2. Practice and discipline

Then Chacha ji said, "Whatever you understand, practice it. Be it math questions or life problems, practice will remove your fear and confusion. Just like Sabu always remains strong with his practice, you too will become expert with practice."

Sabu smiled and said, "Yes, Chacha ji, I too have become strong with practice!"

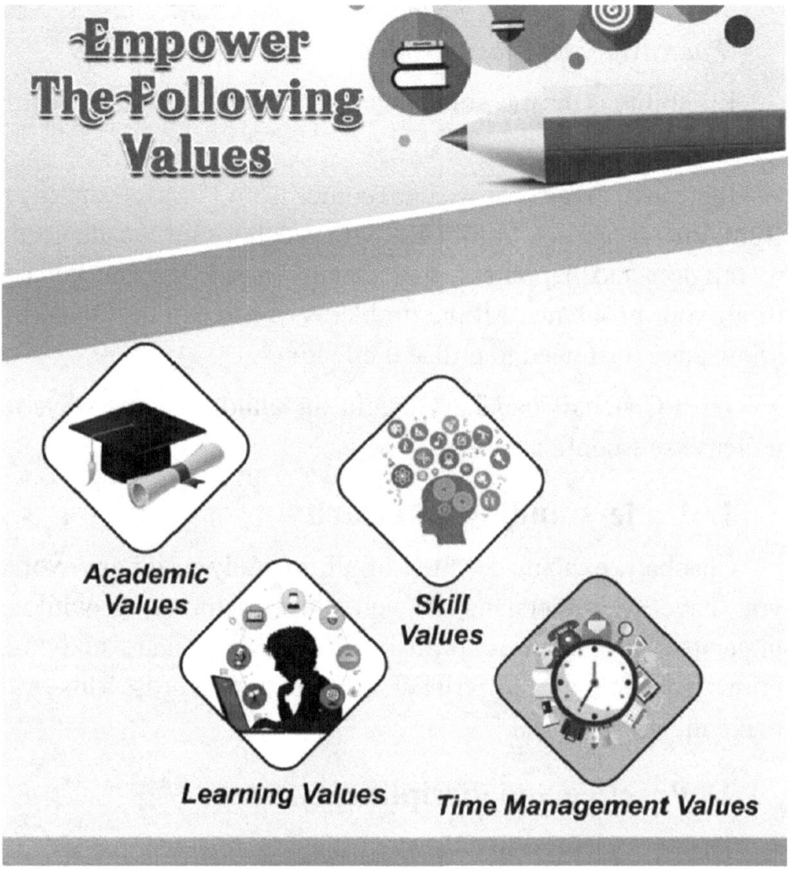
Empower
The Following
Values
Academic
Values
Skill
Values
Learning Values
Time Management Values

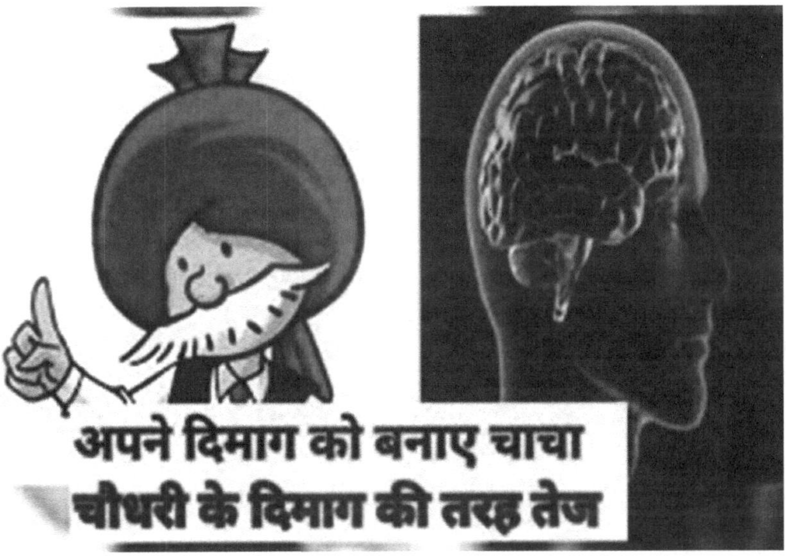
अपने दिमाग को बनाए चाचा
चौधरी के दिमाग की तरह तेज

### 3. Meditation and mental peace

Chacha Chaudhary further said, "If you feel confused, then meditate and take deep breaths. This will calm your mind and increase your confidence. Meditation will clear your mind and any difficulty will seem easy."

### Success with confidence

After a few weeks, when the exam day came, Pinki, Chhotu and Rakesh gave the exam with confidence. Their hard work and understanding made them successful, and they were able to pass the exam without any confusion.

After the exam, the children said to Chacha Chaudhary, "Thank you, Chacha ji! With your teachings, we were able to travel from confusion to self-confidence."

Chacha ji said smilingly, "Remember children, self-confidence is the key that can open the lock of every confusion. Just walk on the right path and never give up."

❒

*Chapter - 5*

# How to make your mind like Chacha Chaudhary?

## Topic 5.1 - General Knowledge according to Chacha Chaudhary The importance of general studies and awareness

One day Chacha Chaudhary, Sabu and Bini Chachi were sitting in the park. Chhotu came running and said, "Chacha ji, I find general knowledge very difficult. So many topics, so much information! How do I remember it?"

Chacha Chaudhary smiled and said, "Chhotu, general knowledge is not difficult, you just need to learn it in the right way. Just like a plant bears fruits if you water it properly, similarly studying becomes easy with the right knowledge."

Bini Chachi said, "I remember that in old times we used to learn a lot from stories and examples. Once King Vikramaditya asked a question in his court: What is the greatest treasure? The answer was - knowledge!" Chacha Chaudhary nodded his head in agreement and said, "Absolutely! Knowledge is the real treasure, and to get it we need a little interest and proper learning. For example, do you know which is the highest peak in India?"

Chhotu hesitated and said, "Mount Everest?"

Sabu laughed and said, "No, Chhotu! Mount Everest is the highest peak in the world, but Kanchenjunga is the highest peak in India."

Chacha Chaudhary explained, "See, this is called *'Aniyamitta Ki samasya'* (Problem of inconsistency). If you read and repeat a little bit of information every day, then it stays in your memory. For example, learn one new thing every day, like which is the largest river in India?"

Chhotu and Sabu said together, "Ganga!"

Chacha Chaudhary praised him and said, "Absolutely right! In this way, when you add a new information to your mind every day, general knowledge becomes easy."

Then Bini Chachi recited a Sanskrit shloka: -

*Na chor haaryam na cha raj haaryam,*
*na bhraatribhajyam na cha bharkari.*
*Vyaye krite vardhat eva nityam,*
*vidyaa dhanam sarvadhanpradhaanam.*

Chacha Chaudhary explained the meaning of the shloka, "Knowledge is such a wealth which no one can steal, nor a king can snatch, nor a brother can divide, nor is it a burden. It increases when spent. That is why knowledge is the greatest wealth."

Sabu said curiously, "Chacha ji, does that mean if we learn a little bit of information every day, then studying will become easy?"

Chacha Chaudhary smiled and said, "Absolutely! The way to make general knowledge easy is to learn it little by little every day. Understand this, mere memorization is not enough."

Chhotu also said enthusiastically, "Now I will learn a new information every day and share it with my friends."

Chacha Chaudhary finally said, "Remember, to expand knowledge, accumulate it gradually and make it a part of your life. Only then will you have a treasure of general knowledge."

## Topic 5.2 - Chacha Chaudhary and the Magic of Innovation

Chacha Chaudhary, Sabu and some children are sitting in the garden. A child asks curiously, "Chacha ji, earlier people used to walk, and now we can fly in an airplane. How did this happen?"

Chacha Chaudhary smiles and says, "Son, all this is the wonder of human thinking and the power of innovation. Until man did not take his thinking out of the limits, he did not get progress. If people kept thinking only about what was in front of them, then we would still be walking on foot."

### Development of means of travel

Chacha Chaudhary explained to the children, "In the beginning, man used to walk only on foot. Then someone thought, 'Why not make something that can travel far faster and with less effort?' This thought led to the invention of the bicycle. Then the motor car, train, and finally the airplane was made. All this happened because someone thought, 'What could be better than this?' And when man thought like this, then new inventions keep happening."

The children asked in surprise, "So was it important to think every time?"

Chacha Chaudhary shook his head and said, "Yes, absolutely. Unless you think what can be done better, there will be no progress."

Chacha Chaudhary then said, "Thomas Edison, who made the electric bulb, failed thousands of times in making it. But he never gave up. Edison said, 'I did not fail, I just learned 10,000 ways that do not work.' It was his fearlessness and his thinking that gave us light."

Sabu jokingly said, "When Edison was making the bulb, I thought he would burn me too!"

All the children started laughing and Chacha Chaudhary said with a light smile, "Yes Sabu, but this was an invention to bring light, not to burn."

Chacha Chaudhary repeated a famous sentence of Aristotle, "A great thinker is the one who takes a step in the direction of new thinking. As long as we keep thinking in the old way, we will never be able to create something new."

The children asked in surprise, "So was Aristotle also an inventor?"

Chacha explained, "Aristotle was a great philosopher, who taught people to think in the new way." I taught them that with the power of thinking and understanding, we can solve any problem."

## Development of Medicine and Science

After this, Chacha Chaudhary told the children how medical science progressed. "Earlier people used to leave diseases to God. Then someone thought, 'Why not find a cure for them?' This thought led to the invention of medicines and treatments. Gradually, science found solutions to diseases and today we can treat even the biggest diseases."

Sabu then joked, "Chacha ji, if I were a doctor, then probably the patients would have been scared of me!"

Chacha Chaudhary said laughingly, "Yes, but you would have made the patients unconscious before treating them!"

**All the children started laughing loudly.**

Finally, Chacha Chaudhary said, "So children, if you want to progress in life, then expand your thinking. Think beyond limits. New ideas and innovations will take you to the heights of success. As Aristotle said, 'The power to think makes a man great.' Until a man has asked questions and tried to change the world around him, no invention has taken place."

The children said excitedly, "We will also invent new things when we grow up and change the world!"

Chacha Chaudhary and Sabu were laughing and listening to the children. The story ends, but a new passion and enthusiasm has awakened in the minds of the children.

## Topic 5.3 - Chacha Chaudhary's Lesson on Time Management and Discipline

One day Chacha Chaudhary was resting in his courtyard, when Pinki and Rakesh came running to him. Both had lines of worry on their faces. Pinki took a deep breath and said, "Chacha ji, nowadays the burden of studies has increased so much that I don't understand how to pass the time. Everyone is expected to score 95%, and even 24 hours of the day are not enough for this!"

Chacha Chaudhary smiled and said, "The problem is not of lack of time, but of time management. Discipline in life and proper time management are the keys to success."

Sabu, who was sitting quietly till now, said, "Chacha ji, this is true, but today's children have a very busy day. They spend 8 hours in school, then 1 hour of coaching, 1 hour of school homework, then 1-2 hours of repeating the coaching lessons. In total, they spend 15 hours only in studies.

And then 8 hours of sleep is also necessary. In this way, they spend 23 hours studying and sleeping. Now they have only 1 hour left for eating, drinking, bathing and other activities. How do they maintain balance in such a situation?"

Chacha Chaudhary shook his head and said, "Everyone has equal time, even if it is 24 hours. But the right use of time makes you different from others. First of all, we have to understand that there is a time for every work. If we do every work at its fixed time, then time management will become easy."

Pinki asked in surprise, "But Chacha ji, how do we find time in the midst of so many tasks?"

## Planning the time

Chacha Chaudhary explained while making a small chart, "Look children, first of all make a schedule of your day. In that, decide which work is to be done when. The most important thing is to set priorities for studies. Give a deadline to every task and complete it accordingly. By working within deadlines, you will always know what to do in a given time and you will never be confused."

## Positive thinking and discipline

Chacha ji further said, "Another important thing is positive thinking and discipline. If you make time your friend and do every task according to its priority, then even 24 hours will seem like a lot to you. Discipline does not only mean doing work on time, but also doing the right thing. If you plan your studies properly, then you will not need to study again and again. If you study once and revise it on time, then it will always be remembered."

Sabu asked, "Chacha ji, has anyone become successful without discipline?"

Chacha Chaudhary smiled and said, "No Sabu! Every successful person has followed discipline in his life. Mahatma Gandhi had said, 'Discipline is the bridge that lies between the goal and its achievement.' If you follow discipline, you can score more than 95% marks."

## Play and rest are also important:

Chacha Chaudhary finally said, "Along with studies, rest and exercise are also important. When your brain gets tired, play for a while, do some physical activity or meditate. This will refresh your brain and you will be able to study with new enthusiasm. Remember, balance is the real key to success."

Rakesh and Pinki nodded their heads and said, "Thank you, Chacha ji! Now we will manage our studies and time properly and score more than 95% marks!"

Chacha Chaudhary smiled and said, "This is the right way, children! Live your time with discipline and success will kiss your feet."

## Topic 5.4 - Mantra to be happy and successful in life

To be happy and successful in life is everyone's wish. We all want to have success along with happiness in our lives. But have you ever wondered what it really means to be happy and successful? Often, we associate success only with high marks, a good career or a fat salary. But in reality, success is incomplete unless it has a tadka of happiness. Happiness and success go hand in hand. If you are happy in life and studies, success comes automatically.

## Importance of happiness

Being happy means that you are enjoying your every day. When we are happy, we are able to concentrate more on our work or studies. Happiness improves our mental health and gives us the strength to face the challenges of life. Therefore, it is very important to keep your mind light and happy while studying or doing any work in life.

When you learn to accept your life and circumstances, you get mental peace. Self-satisfaction teaches us how we can be happy with what we have. When you do your work wholeheartedly and have faith in your abilities, success also kisses your feet. The famous philosopher Aristotle said, “Happiness is not related to what you have, but to the way you live.” If we find satisfaction in every little moment of our life, happiness will always be with us. Another important thing to be happy and successful is the desire to learn new things. When we learn new things, it deepens our understanding and a new energy is generated in our mind. It not only makes our work fun, but also gives us a chance to increase our creativity. When you start enjoying the process of learning, then both success and happiness start coming closer to you. Another secret of a happy and successful life is patience and consistency. Often people are in a hurry and want to get immediate results. But real success is the one that comes with patience.

When you move slowly towards your goal while being stable, success comes closer to you. Confucius said, “It does not matter if you go slowly, as long as you do not stop.” This is also applicable in studies. When you focus on your studies with patience, not only do you understand it better, but you also succeed in it. Now when we talk about creativity, it is also an important part of being happy and successful. Creativity is the solution to every problem in life. Creativity gives us a chance to look at problems from a new perspective and gives a new look to our life. Whether it is studies or any other area of life, when we think creatively, our possibilities increase. Finally, it is also important to talk about self-evaluation. Testing yourself from time to time, learning from your mistakes and recognizing your capabilities is the way you can improve yourself every day.

When you evaluate every aspect of your life correctly, it not only gives you happiness but also success. The most important thing to be happy and successful in life is to know yourself, be kind and empathetic to the people around you, and try to learn something new every day. When we adopt these values in our life, both happiness and success become a part of our life.

"Happiness is the art of being able to live every little moment of life, and success is the science that gives us the opportunity to beautify those moments."

*Thank you for reading and understanding this book.*

*I am sure that by following the ideals of Chacha Chaudhary and using his methods, you too can get a mind like Chacha Chaudhary!*

'Be Intelligent' !!

❑❑❑